Bhavani ☆

Fall 2021

♡ A journey together ♡

BE DEVOTED

"Bob Schuchts provides a beautiful and compelling vision for marriage and sexuality. His honest sharing about his own childhood and marriage, as well as practical tools for reflection and discussion, will equip couples to make real strides toward deeper marital unity."

Peter and Debbie Herbeck
Renewal Ministries

"*Be Devoted* is not just another book about marriage. Bob Schuchts draws upon his own deep experience and the treasure of Catholic theology to offer a tremendous resource to married couples and to the Church. This book, both practical and profound, stands to unlock the full potential of married love to the power of God's healing grace."

Fr. John Burns
Author of *Lift Up Your Heart*

"For years, in our own marriage and in our marriage ministry, we have searched for a marriage book that is both authentically Catholic and powerfully transformational. We have finally found that treasure in *Be Devoted*. Bob Schuchts's knowledge, wisdom, and vulnerability make this an impactful and relatable read. If you are married, preparing for marriage, or simply want to better understand the Sacrament of Marriage, this is the book for you!"

Paul and Gretchen George
Art of Living Ministry

"In *Be Devoted*, Bob Schuchts challenged the two of us with his beautiful and tender reflection about marriage. We loved it and highly recommend it for anyone who is serious about the essential role of the Sacrament of Matrimony in the New Evangelization."

Ryan and Mary-Rose Verret
Founders of Witness to Love

"In *Be Devoted*, Bob Schuchts takes his God-given insights from *Be Healed* and *Be Transformed* and draws them straight into the heart of the home. *Be Devoted* deeply challenged us and invited us to more fully trust Christ with the entirety of our marriage, family, and shared lives. In a culture where marriage and family are under attack, we are in even greater need of Jesus Christ and the healing that he alone can bring. *Be Devoted* is essential reading for any engaged or married couple wanting to live a Christ-centered life together."

Curtis and Michaelann Martin
Founders of FOCUS

"Everyone should read this book. It is not only a practical guide but also a road map for successfully navigating the Sacrament of Marriage. We have offered hope and healing for married couples for the past nineteen years in our apostolate, and this will be our go-to resource from now on."

Greg and Julie Alexander
Founders of *The Alexander House*

"*Be Devoted* is an outstanding book on the power and beauty of two hearts becoming one in the Sacrament of Marriage. This piercingly honest and revealing work, born out of Bob Schuchts's own life and decades of private practice as a marriage and family therapist, will deeply impact your heart and life with its wisdom, grace, and inspiration. We all wish to have a safe place to love and to be loved, and this book points to the ultimate expression of Jesus' deep love and care for each of us. If you are looking to build trust, intimacy, joy, and passion in your marriage, you need this book!"

Sr. Miriam James Heidland, S.O.L.T.
Author of *Loved as I Am*

"This book will be a tremendous gift to all married and engaged couples and those who minister to them."

From the foreword by **Christopher and Wendy West**
Theology of the Body Institute

BE DEVOTED

Restoring Friendship, Passion, and
Communion in Your Marriage

BOB SCHUCHTS

Ave Maria Press AVE Notre Dame, Indiana

Nihil Obstat: Hector R. G. Perez, S.T.D.
                 Censor Librorum
Imprimatur: Most Reverend William A. Wack, D.D., C.S.C.
                 Bishop of Pensacola–Tallahassee
                 Given at Pensacola, FL, on 29 July 2019

The *Nihil Obstat* and *Imprimatur* are official declarations that a book or pamphlet is free of doctrinal or moral error. No implication is contained therein that those who have granted the *Nihil Obstat* or *Imprimatur* agree with its contents, opinions, or statements expressed.

Unless otherwise stated, scripture texts in this work are taken from the *New American Bible, revised edition* © 2010, 1991, 1986, 1970 Confraternity of Christian Doctrine, Washington, DC, and are used by permission of the copyright owner. All rights reserved. No part of the *New American Bible* may be reproduced in any form without permission in writing from the copyright owner.

Foreword © 2019 by Christopher West and Wendy West

Founded in 1865, Ave Maria Press is a ministry of the United States Province of Holy Cross.

www.avemariapress.com

Paperback: ISBN-13 978-1-59471-897-7

E-book: ISBN-13 978-1-59471-898-4

Cover image © iStock / Getty Images Plus.

Cover design by Brian C. Conley.

Text design by Andy Wagoner.

Printed and bound in the United States of America.

Library of Congress Cataloging-in-Publication Data is available.

IN MEMORY OF MY BELOVED WIFE, MARGIE.

As I envision you now in heaven, I see your radiant beauty, living fully as the kind, joyful, and giving person that you are. Every day, I see your reflection in our children and grandchildren. I am eternally grateful to God for bringing you safely into his arms and for the legacy of love you left us.

CONTENTS

FOREWORD

by Christopher and Wendy West

St. John Paul II relentlessly encouraged Catholics to incorporate their lived experience of faith and the Catholic vision of human life and love into their professional endeavors. Our friend Bob Schuchts has done that exceptionally well in his long career as a therapist serving marriages and families, as a teacher and ministry leader, and, of course, in this book, which will be a tremendous gift to married and engaged couples and those who minister to them.

Our mutual love for St. John Paul II and his theology of the body was the catalyst that enabled us to meet Bob in 2006. For some time before that, I (Christopher) had been encountering couples around the country who had received marital healing through Bob's ministry. When I continued hearing about his work, I sensed the Holy Spirit nudging me to befriend Bob, and then soon after, to invite him to teach at the Theology of the Body Institute.

One of the first events we did together was a retreat for married couples. Bob's portion of the teaching that weekend incorporated much of this material in *Be Devoted*. I can attest to its power in bringing transformation to couples, whether they've been married sixty years or they're newly engaged. Bob not only has a comprehensive grasp of Church teaching but also he's able to make it both accessible and applicable in very practical ways. His use of personal, heartwarming stories and his humility in sharing his own weaknesses and failings in marriage make this book all the more relatable and relevant.

I've had the privilege of spending time with Bob's family on various occasions over the years. I was deeply saddened when I heard that his wife, Margie, died suddenly in September of 2017. She was such a kindhearted person, and strikingly different in personality and temperament than Bob. I'm not sure I've ever met a married couple who loved each other so well in their differences. The power of their love in their differences was a witness and inspiration to me in loving Wendy in her differences.

I (Wendy) first met Bob when he stayed in our home after one of Christopher's courses in 2006. Our conversations eventually turned to some difficulties Christopher and I were having in our marriage. I was struck not only by Bob's deep willingness to listen but also by his keen insights. The counsel he provided also proved to be very fruitful in our relationship. That same counsel is mapped out beautifully in this book, and I am confident it will bear great fruit in your life as well.

Together, we want to encourage you to read this book carefully and then put it into practice. St. John Paul II wrote that those who seek the fulfillment of their own human and Christian vocation in marriage are called "first of all" to make the theology of the body the content of their lives and their way of living (see TOB 23:5). Bob has done his readers a tremendous service by helping them in very sound and practical ways to do just that.

INTRODUCTION

Be devoted to one another in love.
—Romans 12:10 (NIV)

Have you ever had a single conversation with your spouse or someone close to you completely change the direction of your life? This book and all that it represents is the fruit of one such interaction with my late wife, Margie, many years ago. The conversation was actually a heated argument during the most tumultuous season of our marriage. By then we had been married twelve years, and everything seemed great on the outside. We were both enjoying our professional careers and had finally been able to purchase our first home in a friendly neighborhood with a great elementary school for our daughters, Carrie and Kristen. Despite these outward signs of happiness, things were not so great for me on the inside. My unhealed wounds and the unresolved conflicts in our marriage, which I will elaborate on throughout the book, led me to withdraw my affections from Margie. Seriously doubting our love for each other, I was terrified that these feelings might one day lead to divorce. Yet I was still trying to assure Margie and convince myself that I was committed to our marriage and family as I had promised on our wedding day. But Margie, seeing right through my façade, understood the condition of my heart better than I did. Never one to mince words, her response was priceless (and the motivation for the title of this book): "I don't want your half-hearted commitment. I want your *devotion*."

Though I tried to justify myself, the truth of her words pierced through my defenses and struck me to the core. At that moment, I realized it wasn't enough to stay married out of fear of causing more pain or out of an obligation to do the right thing. Those were good motives, but not good enough. God was calling me to so much more—to be wholeheartedly devoted to my wife and our children. Yet despite recognizing the truth of her words, I felt completely helpless. Emotionally bankrupt, I was barely holding on during this darkest period of our marriage. I had not yet walked through my much-needed personal healing or discovered many of the life-changing truths I am about to share with you in this book.

Looking back, I realize this was one of the defining moments of my life. My choices would set the future course of our marriage and family life. These decisions would affect me, Margie, our children, and many others for the rest of our lives. I realized, like never before, how much I desperately needed God's help. Though I believed in God, I had largely relied upon myself and on my professional training in marriage matters. But in this moment of heightened awareness, I understood that neither my graduate school training nor my years of experience as a marriage and family therapist were enough. Only God could change my heart and save our marriage.[1]

In the years since that life-changing confrontation, I have had many opportunities to reflect on what it means to *be devoted* as a husband, father, and follower of Jesus Christ. As a culture, we have devalued "devotion," even as we have debased the Sacrament of Matrimony. But devotion can never go out of style, because it is nothing other than genuine love, which every human being needs and ultimately desires. *To be devoted is to know true and lasting love.*

These timeless virtues of passionate love, affection, faithfulness, and dedication are just as essential today as they have ever been. They are fundamental to enjoying a healthy and happy marriage, just as they are to our spiritual well-being. In fact, marital devotion and spiritual devotion go hand in hand. Genuine devotion in marriage is a by-product of our wholehearted devotion to God. The definitions of *devote* tell the story: "to commit by a solemn act,"[2] "to appropriate by . . . a vow; set apart or dedicate by a solemn or formal act; consecrate."[3] All these definitions speak to essential aspects of the Sacrament of Matrimony.[4]

In devoting ourselves to each other in the covenant of marriage, we give up our single life for a greater fulfillment and a greater responsibility. We stand before God and the community to declare our desire and willingness to enter into a new life together. We profess our vows to each other and allow God to strengthen the bond. We ask that God "may mercifully pour out the blessing of his grace and make of one heart in love those he has joined by a holy covenant."[5]

God's faithful and passionate love is mirrored in the synonyms for *devoted*. As you read through these synonyms, I invite you to think about your own marriage (whether past, current, or future), as well as your parents' marriage, to see how well these words describe the quality and nature of each relationship. These synonyms for *devoted* give us a summary of what true love looks like:

* loyal
* faithful
* true
* committed
* devout
* fond
* loving
* affectionate
* caring
* passionate

Whether or not you are married, I suspect these descriptions of devotion express your deepest desires for how you *want* to be loved—by God, your spouse, and anyone else to whom you feel close. Deep down, we all want to be loved and to love in this way—with affection and constancy, with fondness and affection. We want a mutual love that is true and dedicated, but at the same time passionate and intimate. This kind of love expresses God's heart for each one of us. I believe it is also the kind of love he desires for every marriage.

Yet too many of us in this broken world experience the opposite. The following antonyms for *devoted* depict what too many married couples endure—a relationship without love, lacking genuine affection. Again, I invite you to read through these words slowly and remember when you experienced a relationship devoid of devotion and what it felt like. These antonyms speak to the reality of a loveless relationship:

- unloving
- detached
- distant
- hard-hearted
- standoffish
- unbending
- uncaring
- unfeeling
- heartless
- unromantic

I'm ashamed to admit these antonyms for *devoted* described the state of my heart when Margie confronted me. I don't blame her for being angry and calling me to more. Who really wants a relationship like that? No one wants to be married to someone who is heartless and unloving. I don't believe any engaged couple starts off looking for a marriage without devotion. I know we didn't. But tragically, too many relationships end up there. These descriptions reveal a marriage where heartfelt devotion is sorely missing. Sadly, this lack of dedicated love between spouses spreads like a cancer affecting everyone around them. Without devotion, bonds of fear and self-protection replace healthy bonds of love and affection, not only in the marriage but throughout the family as well. Many people are negatively impacted when a married couple is not devoted, first in their relationship with God and then with each other.

As you reflect on your own life history, can you see where you have experienced the fulfillment that comes from devoted love versus the pain that inevitably arises without devotion? I have experienced both realities in my childhood home and in my own marriage, so I know the joy of devoted love and the anguish that comes when it is lacking. I will share more about these experiences throughout the book.

If the synonyms for *devoted* love describe your marriage or your family life growing up, you have been blessed in knowing true love. For you, this book will build on the good foundation that has already been laid while providing insights and practical skills to cultivate an even deeper and more fulfilling intimacy with your spouse and family. It will also help you heal from any past relational hurts that could potentially hinder your love and devotion in the future.

If the antonyms more fittingly describe your marriage, past relationships, or your parents' marriage, you will discover in this book priceless tools to bring deep healing to your broken heart and broken relationships, and to those of your spouse and children while also offering a blueprint for healthy and life-giving marital love.

If you are not yet married but desire to be married soon or in the future, I cannot think of a better way for you to prepare for the kind of relationship that will bring you and your future spouse the insight and skills you need to be devoted to each other for life, and to heal from past and current relational wounds. Today, intimate relationships before marriage can be extremely damaging because many of them lack purity, faithfulness, and devotion. As a result, many couples enter marriage brokenhearted without even knowing it. If this is your situation, you may need time to heal before jumping into another relationship. You must restore your capacity to trust and be intimate, through healing from these past hurts.

If you are currently living together and not married, I encourage you to read this book with the hope of finding what you are really searching for—genuine love. I believe you will discover that the insights and activities contained in this book provide you with the knowledge you need to have the kind of enduring and faithful love you seek.

If you are a pastor, therapist, marriage mentor, teacher, spiritual director, or perhaps a friend of a couple in need of encouragement, you will find in these pages a trustworthy blueprint for how to educate, heal, and support marriages according to God's unfailing and uplifting design.

In my thirty-five years as a marriage and family therapist, I discovered valuable insights about devoted love through the couples and individuals I counseled. I also met with many who were single, celibate, divorced, or widowed. I realized from those varied experiences that we all have similar relational wounds from distorted love. Yet, no matter how badly we have been damaged by false and shallow experiences of "love," we all share an unquenchable thirst for lasting fulfillment in our intimate relationships. If you desire that, no matter what state of life you are in now, I am confident you will find this book to be a valuable source of inspiration and encouragement.

Be Devoted is rooted in the Catholic Church's beautiful and life-giving teachings about relationships. Throughout the book I draw liberally from scripture and Church teaching, especially the writings of St. John Paul II. I will also reference well-respected therapists, researchers, and authors who have written insightful books on relationships and marriage. My intention is to offer you both age-old wisdom and practical tools. For that purpose, every chapter contains activities that will enable you to apply what you are reading to your own life circumstances and relationship.

Since my retirement from private practice as a marriage and family therapist, I have been presenting this material in marriage conferences throughout the United States, through the John Paul II Healing Center. Repeatedly, couples who attend these conferences express how much they have benefitted: "This has changed my understanding of marriage. I wish I had known this before I got married." "This should be required for every couple who gets married in the Church." "This has given me the skills and healing to love my (husband/wife) like I always wanted to." "This is a beautiful vision for marriage. It gives me so much hope." "This saved our marriage." "I have never heard such a beautiful teaching on sexuality." "Every couple could benefit from this teaching."

I realize that these Unveiled conferences (as we call them at the healing center) will only reach a small portion of marriages throughout the world. That is my reason for writing this book. I have a burning desire to pass on the graces I have received. I have a longing to see every marriage formed in God's unfailing truth and healed by his merciful love. I believe this is possible for every couple and for every person who has struggled in any kind of relationship. I have witnessed firsthand in my own marriage, and in the lives of many others, how Jesus' healing love and his eternal truths can transform our lives and relationships. No matter where you are in your life circumstances, I believe this practical guide will be a source of help and encouragement to you personally.

This book is divided into two sections. The first part, "Becoming One," examines how a couple at any age or stage can grow in love and greater intimacy with each other by building a strong marital bond. Following the first two chapters ("Devoted for Life" and "Five Key Areas of Unity"), the next five chapters are organized around each of these five key areas: spiritual unity, emotional intimacy, daily companionship, cooperative teamwork, and sexual fulfillment. Each chapter lays out a blueprint for how to build unity and intimacy in that vital area and then offers reflection questions and short but impactful exercises to practice the necessary skills to foster healthy communication.

Part II, "Healing and Reconciliation" (chapters 8 through 10), provides the necessary understanding and skills to negotiate conflicts in ways that will lead to deeper intimacy. You will also receive the knowledge and practical tools to repair past and present breaches in the relationship, so that wounds can be overcome and transformed into deeper connections with God and each other. Once again, each chapter is followed by reflection questions. The practical activities are designed specifically for married and engaged couples, but they can be beneficial for any relationship.

In addition, at the end of the book, three appendices are provided for practical assistance. Appendix 1 offers an examination for couples that allows you to reflect on how well you are practicing devoted love together daily. Appendix 2 offers prayers for fostering unity in marriage. Finally, appendix 3 provides resources for healing through the John Paul II Healing Center.

Throughout the book I will share many personal experiences from my own marriage and childhood to illustrate how wounds and character weaknesses lead to brokenness in marriage. I will also share the many answers to prayer and the wisdom I received along the way, which not only helped my marriage but has also been a source of encouragement and hope for hundreds of couples.

As you begin this journey, I ask the Holy Spirit to guide and inspire you. May he lead you deeper into union with Christ, so that you will know the joy and security of devoted love.

PART I

BECOMING ONE

1

DEVOTED FOR LIFE

What God has joined together, no human
being must separate.

—Matthew 19:6

As I stood before the altar gazing into my young bride's beautiful blue eyes, my nerves quieted, and I felt a deep peace descend upon me. Tenderly holding her hands and surveying her sweet face, I knew I wanted to spend the rest of my life with this woman whom I loved like no one else on earth. I couldn't wait for her to become my life-long companion and, God willing, the future mother of our children. I longed for us to *be devoted* to each other for the rest of our lives.

In exchanging our sacred vows that day, Margie and I understood that we were giving ourselves in love, establishing an indissoluble union that would last our lifetime. We were promising, before God and all our loved ones, to faithfully *love and cherish each other*, "for better, for worse, for richer, for poorer, in sickness and in health . . . until death do us part."[1]

Standing before the priest and our families and closest friends, who were our witnesses, Margie and I understood that we were pledging to love each other no matter what might transpire in the days, weeks, and years to come. On our wedding day, none of us have any way of knowing how our love will be challenged over the years. We hope we will have good times, good health, and enough resources to care for our material needs. We don't even want to think about the possibility of relational difficulties, sicknesses, or the lack of resources with which we might have to contend. Furthermore, we usually aren't cognizant of how our collective wounds and sins will inevitably make it difficult to love and honor each other the way we promised at the altar. And most of us certainly aren't thinking about that last phrase of our vows: "Until death do us part."

Although marriage requires a daily dying to self-centeredness, I certainly wasn't thinking about death on my wedding day. But that last phrase of our vows—*till death do us part*—means a lot more to me now. A little over a year ago, I had to face the reality of those words as I said goodbye to my lifelong companion. Looking back on our nearly forty-two years of marriage, I realize we experienced all the ups and downs mentioned in our vows. We shared some joyously good times and some painfully difficult ones. At times we loved and served each other admirably; at other times we were more selfish and neglected each other's needs. We were financially poor for our first several years while I went to graduate school and started my career. But we always had enough to cover our needs. Though we had a modest income by American standards, we were well-off in comparison to most of the world. We had ample resources, and in the end we were rich in the things that matter most: a life-giving relationship with God, beautiful children and grandchildren, a loving family, meaningful work, trustworthy friends, and a supportive community.

During most of our years together, Margie and I were both in relatively good physical health, apart from an occasional cold or seasonal influenza. But then a year and a half ago (as of this writing), Margie was diagnosed with the sporadic form of a rare, degenerative neurological disease, Creutzfeldt-Jakob disease. CJD affects one in a million people in the United States each year and eats away at the proteins in the brain causing rapid decline in both cognitive and physical capabilities (including dementia, loss of ability to walk and talk, and diminished motor-skill coordination). Like most people who are diagnosed with this disease, Margie's capacities deteriorated progressively. Within four months after her first visible symptoms, she passed away. Despite her physical and mental decline, we intimately experienced God's presence.

In the words of Charles Dickens's famous novel *A Tale of Two Cities*, "They were the best of times and the worst of times." Far sooner than any of us expected, our marriage vows had reached their culmination.

Ups and Downs of Marriage

I entered our marriage with the full intention of being devoted to Margie for life. I had witnessed and experienced my parents' divorce, which added to my determination to have a good marriage that lasted a lifetime. I believe Margie entered our sacrament with the same desires, but without the fearful intensity I brought into it, since her parents remained married for more than sixty years.

On our wedding day, Margie and I both desired to be happily married and to share the overflow of our love with our future offspring and extended families. Though we have had many joyful seasons and beautiful memories, our marriage was not a storybook romance by any stretch of the imagination. When we were first married, we were both largely unaware of how each of our unhealed wounds and habitual patterns of self-centeredness would compromise and eventually threaten our love for each other. After the first few years of marriage, we began to drift apart. Our hearts became nearly deaf to God's voice and numb to each other's pain. Wounds brought into our marriage were compounded by the many ways we continued to hurt each other on a daily basis. In response, I became emotionally distant and slowly withdrew my affections, without fully realizing the damage this was causing Margie and our two beautiful daughters, Carrie and Kristen, who were preteens at the time.

Though I remained faithful to Margie outwardly, my lack of devotion to her soon became evident to both of us. Unresolved conflicts, unrepented sins, and unaddressed wounds led us both to pull back in self-protection during this difficult time. Haunted by the thought that I had fallen out of love, I became vulnerable to almost incessant temptations to deny our sacred vows and divorce the one to whom I had tenderly spoken my promise of unconditional love. I lost sight of her goodness and beauty and began to rationalize and justify my lack of affection. Ironically, while overly preoccupied with her faults and failings, I remained largely blind to my own.

This time of great testing in our marriage reached a crisis point when I turned thirty-three years old—the same age as my parents when they separated. Our children were around the same age I was when I lost contact with my dad for several years. To my dismay, I found myself living through my worst nightmare—and bringing my wife and children into it—against their will. To paraphrase Yogi Berra, it was déjà vu all over again. Yet despite my lack of emotional connection with Margie, I knew that I could not take lightly my sacred vows, since they were made before God and our family and friends. It was during this season of our marriage that Margie's confrontation over my lack of devotion became a catalyst for much-needed changes in my life. Feeling trapped, I prayed in earnest like never before.

Calling Out to God

Every night, after tucking Carrie and Kristen into bed, I would close the door to our bedroom and call out to God in desperation. I hadn't yet faced the unhealed wounds from my parents' divorce. But I knew I didn't want to cause my wife, our children, and myself the same kind of pain and damage that my parents, siblings, and I experienced. At the same time, I couldn't see any other way out of this nightmare. I felt completely out of control, as evidenced by having panic attacks for the first time in my life, whenever I thought of the possibility of divorce. Only now, in retrospect, can I see the Father's providential care for us throughout this time, bringing my wounds to the surface so that I could be devoted to him and to Margie the way I desired.

God initially answered my prayers through a neighbor who invited me to a Bible study with a small group of men. At the first meeting, I listened as one of the men read this passage from scripture: "Because you are lukewarm, neither hot nor cold, I will spit you out of my mouth" (Rv 3:16). As he read these words aloud, it seemed as though Jesus himself spoke them directly to me. Apparently, Jesus didn't appreciate my half-hearted commitment any more than Margie did.

Stunned by the force of his words, I left the meeting with heightened anxiety. After reflecting on what transpired, I realized that the Holy Spirit was showing me that my marriage to Margie was a mirror reflection of my relationship with Jesus. Until that moment, I hadn't realized that the deeper issue in our marriage was within me, rooted primarily in my lack of devotion to Jesus. I had retreated to my intellect to protect my heart from the pain of my parents' divorce. I couldn't love Margie and our daughters well unless I first opened my heart to Jesus' love and devoted myself wholeheartedly to him in return.

These shocking realizations prompted me to engage in some serious soul-searching. Jesus' confrontation, like Margie's earlier one, ended up changing the trajectory of our marriage, as well as our children's lives. The changes in me and in our marriage were slow at first. But progressively, the Holy Spirit led me through a process of healing to address the long-ignored wounds from my childhood and adolescent years—and to confront my pride, which had kept these wounds hidden from my sight.

Healing in Marriage

Healing is a process. As you will read in the chapters to come, Margie and I continued to heal, to reconcile, and to learn what it means to be devoted to each other right up to the final months of her life. Our healing was not a quick fix, although there were certain turning points that gave us additional strength to continue walking in the right direction. In the end, we shared a beautiful intimacy with God, with each other, and with our children and grandchildren. Our family and friends could see the fruit of what God had done in our marriage, in and through our many struggles. A few months before Margie died, her sister Ann remarked, "I am touched to see you both so deeply in love with each other, even more than when you first met."

Throughout our marriage together, we enjoyed many memorable moments. But few were as impactful as those we experienced during those last months of Margie's life. One of my many cherished

memories came in the last weeks of Margie's life as we spontaneously reaffirmed our wedding vows. The occasion was inspired by our
daughter Kristen and son-in-law Stephen returning from his parents'
fiftieth wedding anniversary. As they were sharing about Stephen's
parents reaffirming their vows, Margie perked up, looked at me, and
lucidly stated, "I want to do that." I was delighted she wanted to, because she had often resisted doing so in the past when I suggested it.
Even more, I was amazed at her ability to process the conversation so
cogently despite her compromised ability to articulate her thoughts.

As I knelt in front of Margie in the wheelchair, I looked into her
beautiful blue eyes. The tender look on her face reminded me of our
wedding day. I began with a proposal: "Will you marry me?" With
childlike innocence, she responded with the sweetest smile and a de-
cisive yes. Tears sprang to both of our eyes, as well as our daughter
Kristen's. A few seconds later, with tears flowing freely, I reaffirmed
our sacred vows, which had given us the grace to persevere through
all our challenges. Slowly emphasizing each phrase, I repeated the
words from our wedding day: "I, Bob, take you, Margie, . . . for better,
for worse, for richer, for poorer, in sickness and in health, to love and
to cherish until death do us part."

Reaffirming our vows this final time impacted us both profoundly, even more than when we professed them on our wedding day.
Through the years, in the face of our trials, our love had matured. It
had now reached its culmination. Staring death in the face, we were
no longer afraid of our weaknesses and failures. We knew that our
love, strengthened by God's grace, had finally proven to be stronger
than death (see Sg 8:6).

As I consciously restated these vows one last time, I could see how
God's love had been perfected in our weaknesses. I finally came to
terms with my limitations as a husband and Margie's shortcomings as
a wife. We gave what we were each capable of giving, as best as we
could, considering our limitations. His mercy and grace made up for
what we lacked. In the end, I handed Margie over to Jesus, knowing
that he was her *True and Eternal Bridegroom*—knowing he loved her
the way I always wanted to but never fully could. My love for Margie

was temporal and marred by my wounds, sins, and selfishness. Jesus' love, by contrast, is perfect and eternal. I realized in that moment that our marriage, though vitally important to our salvation and the source of much fruitfulness, was an imperfect representation of our eternal marriage that will reach its perfection in heaven.

I share these details of our marital history as an invitation for you to reflect on your own. I encourage you to look back upon (or forward to) your wedding day. Think about the meaning of your wedding vows and the vicissitudes of life that you will continue to encounter in the future. And though it is challenging, contemplate that moment when you will say goodbye to each other and one of you will hand the other to Jesus in preparation for the eternal wedding.

With all that in mind, I invite you to take a moment to reflect on the history and future of your marriage. (If you have never been married, use this as an opportunity to reflect on your future marriage or your relationship with God and others.)

Take a Moment

1. What about my story shed light on your personal history and marriage relationship?

2. If today was the last day of your marriage (or life), would you be fulfilled and feel satisfied? What would you regret? What would you be grateful for?

3. What was your intention when you spoke your wedding vows (or baptismal vows/ordination or religious vows)? What do they mean to you now?

Covenant Love

We can only know true love by understanding God's covenant love for us. I am convinced that our greatest happiness is realized in coming to appropriate these deepest truths of our relationship with him. Take to heart these words revealed through the Old Testament prophets to describe God's promise of intimate and unrelenting love for each one of us individually and for us collectively: "I will betroth you to me forever: . . . I will betroth you to me with fidelity, and you shall know the LORD (Hos 2:21–22). "As a bridegroom rejoices in his bride so shall your God rejoice in you" (Is 62:5). "I swore an oath to you and entered into covenant with you . . . and you became mine" (Ez 16:8b).

Have you ever really pondered these images of God as your Bridegroom claiming you as his own, delighting in you and promising his fidelity to you? This imagery becomes even more concrete in the New Testament with the revelation of Jesus as our eternal Bridegroom. Jesus' heartfelt devotion for his bride (the Church) is the pattern God has established for every marriage (see Eph 5:21–32). Through him and in him, we come to a fuller understanding of God's limitless love for us. The nature and extent of this love is revealed throughout the Bible. Numerous passages reveal that Jesus, our Bridegroom, loves us with perfect devotion; *freely* (see Jn 10:18); *fully* (see Jn 15:13); *faithfully* (see 2 Tm 2:13); and *fruitfully* (see Jn 15:5).

Only in considering Jesus' love for each of us can we understand God's full intention for marital love. If you are married, or planning to marry, your wedding vows are among the most important words you will have ever spoken (second only to your baptismal vows). They are your personal pledge to love your spouse with Jesus' covenant love, through the power of the Holy Spirit, *freely, fully, faithfully,* and *fruitfully*.[2] These sacred vows bind you together as husband and wife through all the challenges and hardships of life. Moreover, they are a living sign to the rest of the world of Jesus' covenant love for his Bride.

The world sorely needs this authentic witness of Christ's love revealed in holy marriage. But we know that in our human weakness (sin, wounds, and selfishness), we all fall short. That is why we desperately need his mercy and grace to sustain us. Only by keeping Jesus as our standard of truth and source of strength can we clearly see the nature of covenant love. I have come to realize that we love our spouses to the extent to which Jesus is the primary object of our devotion. Fr. Julián Carrón explains why this is so: "If you do not love Christ, Beauty made flesh, more than the person you love, the latter relationship withers, because Christ is the truth of this relationship, the fullness to which both partners point, and in whom their relationship is fulfilled. Only by letting him in is it possible for the most beautiful relationship that can happen in life not be corrupted and die in time."[3]

I had to come to terms with these eternal realities the hard way. My hope is that you can learn from my experience and from the teachings of the Church what I discovered along the way. This Christian vision of love and marriage stands in stark contrast to the counterfeit "loves" of this world, to which we have all been overexposed through novels, magazines, movies, television shows, and most of our interactions in life. This worldly love is not really love at all. It is a thin disguise for lust. It does not give freely, fully, faithfully, or fruitfully. Rather, it takes from the other and uses the other person as an object for self-gratification and selfish gain, and then discards them when they are no longer useful or desirable.

Unlike the authentic life-giving love that Jesus models, worldly love is based in seduction, manipulation, and coercion (as opposed to loving freely). It is epitomized by grasping and self-centeredness (rather than loving fully). This counterfeit love is marked by infidelity and perversion (rather than loving faithfully). Finally, it is evidenced in contraception and abortion (as opposed to loving fruitfully). Because of original sin, we are all prone to relating to one another in these selfish ways. Tragically, many in today's culture have almost completely lost sight of true love and have been seduced by the cultural counterfeits.

This is precisely why being devoted in love is so vitally important. Our sacred vows rescue us from a world of misery while also providing an authentic witness to the world of true and lasting love. We are promising to love each other with the purest love of Christ, made possible only through our ongoing yielding to the Holy Spirit. This is for our own good, for the good of our children, and for the benefit for the entire body of Christ, as well as the world.[4] True love makes marriage sacred—it transcends the deficient "loves" of this world and elevates marriage to a living expression of Jesus' free, full, faithful, and fruitful love. If we have eyes to see, all this is represented beautifully in the symbolism of a Christian wedding ceremony.

Wedding Symbolism

The traditional Christian wedding ceremony is rich with symbolism, pointing simultaneously to the love between husband and wife while signifying the ultimate marriage of Christ and his Church. According to the imagery employed by St. Paul, every groom is called to be a living icon of Jesus Christ (see Eph 5:25). This means that at every truly Christian wedding, we can look at the groom and see a visible representation of an eternal mystery: Jesus offering himself in covenant as a living sacrifice for his bride. Note that the groom is ordinarily standing before the altar, the place of Jesus' sacrifice. Have you ever wondered why the groom is traditionally dressed in black and wears a white shirt? Black symbolizes his dying with Christ; white is meant to symbolize his purity of heart. (I didn't understand this at the time of my marriage and wore a tan tuxedo instead.)

While the bridegroom stands at the front of the church, the bride ordinarily remains veiled from sight in the back of the church. One of the most suspenseful moments of any wedding is the time of revelation, when the groom first lays eyes on his radiant bride. Traditionally the bride is dressed in all white as a symbol of her purity, because she is called to represent the Bride of Christ "*in splendor, without spot or wrinkle or any such thing, that she might be holy and without blemish*" (Eph 5:27, emphasis added). She is a living representation of the beautiful and holy Church prepared for Christ at the end of time.

For any bride brought up in the Church, this would not be her first time wearing a white "wedding" dress. Most likely, she wore an immaculate white gown on the day of her Baptism as well as the day of her First Communion. In Baptism, she was cleansed by "*the bath of water with the word*" (Eph 5:26, emphasis added). In First

Communion, she received a foretaste of the ultimate communion at the "*wedding day of the Lamb*" (Rv 19:7, emphasis added).

Do you see how important it is for both bride and groom to be in a state of grace as they prepare to be married? We are literally called to signify the purest love between Christ and his Church. No matter how impure we have become due to our false loves up until that moment, the Sacrament of Reconciliation is available as a way of cleansing and healing us before we enter Holy Matrimony. (I regret that I did not fully appreciate this reality when Margie and I were married—it would have saved us a lot of heartache.)

In many Christian weddings, the bride's father is the one to walk his daughter down the aisle. The aisle represents our life journey, preparing us for our marriage to Christ at the end of time. Human fathers represent the Fatherhood of God, who prepares the Bride of Christ before handing her over as a gift to his Beloved Son. Mothers represent Mary, who gives her son away at the Cross. Fathers and mothers have a responsibility before God to prepare their sons and daughters for marriage, to protect their purity, and to teach them by word and example what it means to love authentically.

As the father of our two daughters, I remember vividly those moments walking each of them down the aisle. It is hard to express the range of emotions that I felt offering my daughters (Carrie and Kristen) as precious gifts to their husbands (Duane and Stephen). It was both a sobering time of letting go and a joyful celebration. In some ways, the letting go resembled my handing Margie to her eternal Bridegroom at the end of her life. A whole lifetime of prayers and desires for our daughters came to culmination in those moments. Their mom and I had prepared them, prayed for them, and prayed for their husbands since the day they were born. Now it was finally time to release them, because "a *man shall leave [his] father and [his] mother and be joined to his wife, and the two shall become one flesh*" (Eph 5:31, emphasis added).

This symbolism of handing over in the wedding ceremony reflects a deeper reality. Just as we must let go of our attachments to the world to be married to Christ, so too must every bride and groom be free of any competing attachments to be able to love their spouse above all others.[5] Similarly, parents must release their children so they can be fully joined to their spouses and become one with them.[6] Otherwise the newly married couple would remain tied to their parents in an unhealthy way and not be able to give themselves freely and fully in marriage. (I learned this lesson the hard way because I did not fully separate from my mom and she did not fully let go of me, as I was her first married son whom she depended upon when my dad left.)

Letting go in this way is a very vulnerable time for parents and children alike. As I stood representing my wife, Margie, I formally gave our daughters to their husbands at the front of the altar. I was entrusting our future sons (through marriage) with the most precious gifts that their mother and I could ever give. It was a great risk, but we did so with a certain confidence, trusting that they had been prepared well by us, their families, and by the Church for this moment. Knowing that our daughters and sons-in-law were marrying in the Church gave us great assurance. They understood the sacredness of their wedding vows and were entering marriage with the right intentions.

Right Intentions

The Church, guided for more than two thousand years by the Holy Spirit, realizes that true love must be safeguarded against all the cultural counterfeits. Christian marriage is sacred because it is a sign and embodiment of Christ's own covenant love for us. That is why before any couple can be married in the Church, both husband and wife must understand without ambiguity exactly the kind of love and devotion they are promising God and each other. Individually, they must affirm their *intentions* to be joined to each other in a holy covenant. They must promise God and the Church they will freely, fully, and faithfully devote themselves to each other for a lifetime and remain open to children as the bountiful fruitfulness of their love.

To ensure every couple has these intentions, the Catholic Church requires every married couple to answer these queries in the affirmative before blessing their wedding vows:

"Have you come here to enter into marriage without coercion, freely and wholeheartedly?" (The promise to love *freely*.)

"Are you prepared, as you follow the path of Marriage, to love and honor each other for as long as you both shall live?" (The promise to love *fully* and *faithfully*.)

"Are you prepared to accept children lovingly from God and to bring them up according to the law of Christ and his Church?" (The promise to love *fruitfully*.)

Do you see how these intentions mirror Jesus' free, full, faithful, and fruitful love for his Bride? Fundamentally, these intentions protect the integrity of marriage as a sacramental sign and incarnation of Christ's holy love. They also call each spouse to transcend their self-centered nature in order to be truly devoted to each other for life. These promises, made to the Church, precede the vows that are spoken to each other. They give concrete expression to the vows and ensure true love will be safeguarded, for their mutual good, for the good of their children, and for the good of the entire Church.[7]

In the words of Deacon James Keating: "Ultimately God wants you to fall in love with your spouse in the manner that he loves you: out of sheer gift and in wonder over the beauty of who you are."[8] This is the nature of true love—it delights in the goodness and beauty of the beloved and joyfully sacrifices for the well-being of the other, as Christ has done for us. There is a lot here to digest that is vitally important for your marriage. Before going to the next chapter, take a moment to reflect and discuss how this applies to you and to your marriage. If you are married or engaged, I also encourage you to share in the couple activity together with your spouse or fiancé.

Take a Moment

These can be answered individually, as a couple, or in a group discussion.

1. Do you believe a devoted relationship with Jesus is critical for a good marriage? Why or why not?

2. Are you staying true to your stated intentions that you promised your spouse before God and the Church during your wedding? Where are you not living them as you promised?

3. What parts of the Christian wedding ceremony symbolism caught your attention? How do you relate to it?

Activity for Couples: Sharing of Desires

Write down your answers separately and then share them with each other.

1. On the day of your wedding, what did (do) you desire for your life together? How have your desires changed and matured since then?

2. What do you believe God desired (and desires now) for your marriage?

3. How well are you living each of the four characteristics of covenant love (free, full, faithful, and fruitful) in your marriage (or preparation for marriage)? Which area needs the most improvement?

2

FIVE KEY AREAS OF UNITY

The two shall become one flesh.
—Ephesians 5:31

At the end of the last chapter I encouraged you to reflect upon your personal desires for marriage. Did you discover that you and your spouse (or fiancé) have much in common when it comes to what you truly desire for your marriage? I would imagine you both have a desire to feel connected, to be understood, to be honored, and to be fully and faithfully loved. I also imagine you both want to love each other in these ways. No matter how much you may have buried these desires because of past hurts and disappointments, they persist, because they are a fundamental part of your nature.

We are all born with an unquenchable desire for *communion*. Isn't this one of the underlying reasons you married? God placed these desires in your heart. He wants you and your spouse to enjoy a nourishing intimacy with each other, even more than you desire these things for yourselves. The Church teaches that God intended all relationships, and in a particular way, marriage to be a participation in his own *intimate communion of love*: "God's very being is love. . . . God himself is an eternal exchange of love, Father, Son, and Holy Spirit, and he has destined us to share in that exchange" (*CCC* 221).

Because we are made in the image and likeness of God, "who is love," love is our primary vocation. Yet these desires for love and communion are often frustrated in our daily interactions. Living in this broken world, with all its disordered desires, we can too easily lose sight of God's intention for marriage, and thus bury our deepest desires. As our vision for authentic love becomes distorted and disappointed, we eventually lose hope. This is the situation of many in our culture today. That is why the whole world needs to be restored in understanding God's original plan for unity in marriage.

Original Unity

Pope John Paul II wrote his masterpiece, *Man and Woman He Created Them: The Theology of the Body*, as an answer to the world's confusion about sexuality and relationships. In it, he provides a comprehensive explanation of God's plan for human flourishing, based entirely on holy scripture, and in light of Christian philosophy and Church teaching. He offers a detailed description of God's intention and desire for our humanity and for marriage. Envisioning our existence before sin entered the world, John Paul II speaks of marriage as a deeply fulfilling communion between man and woman, as an expression of their union with God. He refers to this primordial state of marriage as "original unity."[1]

Drawing upon these insights from our namesake, our marriage conferences at the John Paul II Healing Center usually begin with a visual demonstration, depicting this original unity of man and woman with the Trinity at the dawn of creation. (This may sound impossible to demonstrate, but it is a profound experience for many because the Holy Spirit is at work revealing the deeper desires of our hearts.)

We begin the demonstration by inviting three people to represent the Holy Trinity, and then we ask a married couple to represent Adam and Eve in "original unity." Those representing the Father, Son, and Holy Spirit are instructed to form a circle of love, signifying the boundless affection and eternal communion that exists among the three persons of the Trinity. The married couple is then invited to stand in the middle of this all-embracing circle of love.

Immersed in the love of the Trinity, the couple awakens to their natural desire for intimacy and communion. As they spontaneously embrace each other, many are moved to tears, realizing that their hearts have been yearning for this secure intimacy their entire lives and in their marriage. Afterward, many who experience this level of communion (as Adam and Eve) report feeling intense joy. They speak of feeling deep peace and security from being so completely loved by their spouse while surrounded by the strong and tender love of the Trinity.

Those standing in for Adam and Eve are not the only ones deeply touched by the demonstration. Those representing the Trinity, as well as many others who observe this human drama, are equally moved. Though I have watched this demonstration many times, I am personally impacted by it each time. I never tire of seeing the joy and fulfillment of those who participate, as well as many who observe. This demonstration speaks to our universal need for genuine love and intimacy. Deep down, we all want to experience the joy of being completely and securely loved by our spouses while enjoying the interior freedom to love them back with heartfelt trust and devotion. This is because the desire for communion with God and for true love is written in every human heart (see *CCC* 27).

Yearning for Communion

I am convinced that every one of us, no matter our state in life, shares this deep yearning for intimate communion. I first began to reflect on this universal longing while working on my master's thesis in graduate school about forty years ago. I decided to focus my research on Marriage Encounter, a marital enrichment program in the Catholic Church. The program has universal appeal because it helps couples reenvision their marriage as an intimate communion with God and each other. It also provides practical communication skills, called *dialogue*, as a way of strengthening their daily unity. As part of my research, I reviewed a wide range of marriage enrichment programs, including one article that captured my attention and left a lasting impression. The essay was written by David R. Mace, who served with his wife, Vera, as copresident of the National Association of Marriage Enrichment. His article described how unity and intimacy can be sustained in marriage. The title, "Relationship-in-Depth," is what caught my attention, because it speaks about our universal longing for communion in marriage.

In this article and many of his subsequent books, Mace describes a *relationship-in-depth* as the outcome of many years of "communication-in-depth." He highlights several things that are necessary for couples to develop lasting intimacy and unity in marriage, including many of the things we will be addressing throughout this book. However, he cautioned that relationship-in-depth is not a short-term project in marriage. Rather, according to Mace, it is an endeavor that takes a lifetime of covenant love and quality communication between husband and wife. To my dismay, he noted that it takes about *fifty years* to develop this level of unity in marriage.

Having been married only two years at the time of reading Mace's article, I lamented that Margie and I had forty-eight more years to go. I was afraid we would never achieve a relationship-in-depth. And in a sense, my concerns were validated. With Margie dying before we reached our golden anniversary, we didn't fully experience the longevity or depths of relationship that Mace held out as the ideal. But after each decade of marriage, the memory of Mace's wisdom became more and more encouraging to me.

Though my desire for greater communion never wavered, my patience and understanding grew considerably over the years. I realized that Margie and I were both limited in our capacity to love fully. I also realized marriage was not a sprint but a marathon. I needed to be patient with myself, with her, and with our marriage, allowing us both to grow and mature into a greater intimacy. This, after all, is the nature of true love as described by St. Paul: "Love is patient. . . . It . . . hopes all things, endures all things" (1 Cor 13:4, 7).

When I look back over all the years of our marriage, I see many ways and moments in which Margie and I shared beautiful and intimate communion with each other and with our daughters and extended family, including those treasured last months and days of her life. Yet there were also many other days when we each felt lonely, when our desires for intimacy and unity were never fully satisfied within our relationship. I believe this is true for all marriages, to one degree or another. Anyone who has been married for any length of time realizes that neither person in the relationship is capable, apart from God, to love as God loves. So we are each left with unsatisfied longings for intimacy that only He can completely fill. Christopher West, known for his popularization of St. John Paul II's theology of the body, refers to this gap between our desires and their fulfillment as the universal *ache* we all experience.[2]

Yet even though we fall short, those who aim for the goal are much more likely to find fulfillment and unity in marriage than those who suppress their desires and give up hope altogether. The world seems largely to have given up hope that lasting communion is possible. That is why many settle for temporary experiences of superficial intimacy and serial relationships. Others remain "committed," but resign themselves to a marriage without unity or intimacy—what Marriage Encounter refers to as *Married Singles*. Neither of these distortions of relationship are what God intended from the beginning. Rather, God ordained a covenant so we could live in communion.

Covenant and Communion

Recently I had an opportunity to observe how the values of covenant and communion transcend cultural and religious differences. While sitting next to a couple from India on an airplane, the husband and I began to discuss our families. At first I thought our understanding of marriage would be worlds apart (literally and figuratively), since he practiced the Hindu religion and told me he and his wife had an arranged marriage. But by the end of our conversation, I was amazed to discover how much we had in common.

He and his wife had been married for forty-two years (like Margie and I would have been). They also, like us, had two grown children who were married and had children themselves. Furthermore, like Margie and me, this man and his wife were very close to their children, their children's spouses, and their grandchildren. He told me that he and his wife, and their married children, considered their unions to be unbreakable bonds in the eyes of God. He said, "It all comes down to love." He lamented the many casual relationships and breakups creating so much damage in our modern culture.

I was encouraged to hear how important marriage is for this Hindu man and his wife. As we spoke, I also thought of how central the understanding of covenant is within all the major world religions, especially Jewish, Muslim, and Christian faiths. In fact, as we were speaking, I thought about how covenant and communion are the overarching themes that run throughout Bible, which theistic religions refer to in one way or another. Communion is the primary nature of relationship. It is what gives us a sense of belonging and connection. And to survive, it must be protected by covenant—the bond that holds a relationship together and allows unity to flourish.

We see the importance of covenant and communion by looking at relationships that are forged without a covenant. Think for a moment about the quasi-marital relationships in our culture. There are many examples of relationships that seek some level of communion without the protection afforded by covenant: one-night stands, premarital sex, adulterous relationships, cohabitation, serial marriages, and so on. All are ways of enjoying sexual intimacy without safeguarding the relationship and the tender hearts of those involved.

We know from experience how relationships turn out when there is no covenant to protect the vulnerability that is required for this level of intimacy. Though these fragile relationships may start with great passion and a genuine desire for unity, they inevitably end with a trail of broken hearts, not only for the couple but equally so for those who are dependent on them (especially children). Broken relationships, and the broken hearts that inevitably follow, make it more difficult to trust love in future relationships.

Equally troubling are those superficial marriages that establish a covenant bond in name only without any real communion, like those who are baptized but don't actively participate in their faith.[3] These unions are false witnesses to the Sacrament of Marriage. They eventually become empty-shell marriages, in which no genuine intimacy can develop because authentic love is missing. Living in this kind of environment is like living in a desert without water. Without communion, hearts become closed and love disappears.

Deep down, none of us wants either a broken relationship or a shallow, superficial relationship with our spouse. We long for a relationship-in-depth marked by both covenant and communion (i.e., true devotion). For this, we need what Dr. Mace describes as *communication-in-depth*.

Communication-In-Depth

The word *communication* literally means the "process of becoming one." If you enter a sacramental marriage, you legally and mystically become one the moment you consummate your marriage in the sexual embrace. You establish a holy covenant and enter the process of growing in communion. This communion must be fed and nurtured daily by the kind of communication that enables unity to grow and develop over time. Communication is far more than the words we speak. It involves all the ways we express ourselves and even the ways we fail to respond to our spouse.

Researchers say that less than 10 percent of communication is through words; the other 90 percent includes nonverbals such as context, tone of voice, facial expressions, body posture, touch, and so forth.[4] Each of these forms of expression is fundamentally influenced by our attitudes of love and honor for each other, or the lack thereof. When communication is rooted and grounded in covenant love, honesty permeates the relationship, allowing trust to develop organically. Unity naturally flourishes in this kind of nurturing environment. In contrast, when judgments and dishonor prevail, self-expression ceases to be life-giving and instead becomes divisive and destructive. Dr. John Gottman, who spent his career studying the ways couples communicate, concludes that "understanding, honor, and respect" for each other and for marriage are the key ingredients for a long-lasting relationship.[5] Isn't this what we pledge to each other when we publicly profess our wedding vows? But few of us have perfected these virtues in our daily interactions. I now realize that I wasn't mature or healed enough to translate the vows I promised to Margie at our wedding into my daily communication with her. My experience as a marital therapist assured me that I was not alone. I found that very few couples have the spiritual and emotional maturity or communication skills to build lasting unity in their marriages.

Many of us think we are communicating when in fact we are doing the opposite. Much of the time our interactions do not increase our sense of communion; instead, they have the opposite effect. For example, when we demean our spouse or try to use our words and actions to coerce them to do something we want, we end up creating more distance in our relationship. This kind of interaction inevitably causes a breakdown in trust. At these times, our interactions and in-actions foster distance and division rather than strengthen the bonds of unity. Only genuine and consistent love, expressed in our daily communication, can cultivate lasting unity.

When I review the history of my relationship with Margie, I can see times when we were communicating with love and honor and growing closer together as a result. But there were other times when our way of relating created more distance between us. Early in our marriage, and even before we were married, I had an ideal in my mind of what I thought marriage should be. This ideal was distorted by my unhealed wounds and self-reliance. Without realizing it, I expected Margie to fulfill my perfect vision for marriage, even though I hadn't communicated this vision to her clearly. My ideal was good overall, but it was based only partly in faith. Fear was also a major motivator.

My attempt to influence Margie to live up to my ideal was not life-giving for either one of us. I would use my words and actions to persuade her to conform to my vision. My desires for intimacy and unity were somewhat healthy, but my interactions created more distance between us. I wondered why she put up walls and withdrew her heart, and why she couldn't see my needs during those times. It took me a while to realize my way of communicating revealed a deeper problem.

The real problem underlying my poor communication was rooted in my failure to fully cherish Margie. At times, I lacked honor and respect for her personal dignity and free choice, especially when I didn't approve of her decisions or behavior. This lack of honor had even deeper roots, stemming from my lack of honor for my mother and father after their divorce and from broken relationships with girlfriends in my teenage years. Ultimately, this attitude of disrespect was rooted in my own shame, coming out of my lack of submission to God and his covenant. All this is a by-product of original sin. And it was hard for me to acknowledge, because my overall posture was one of honor and respect for Margie, my parents, and everyone else. But even today, there are areas of my heart (and probably yours too) that have not yet been formed in love.

No one wants to be coerced into changing to fit someone else's ideal. This is a violation of our dignity as persons and a betrayal of true love. When we feel pressured by our spouse to think or act in a certain way, we naturally put up walls and pull away in self-protection. Unity only develops when self-giving love is manifested. Slowly, as I matured in love, I learned to honor Margie's freedom and focused on meeting her needs rather than insisting that she meet my needs and my ideals. I also learned to share my needs more vulnerably, as well as my perceptions and experiences, so that she could understand my desires. I also grew in my ability to listen to her perceptions and experiences to discover her needs and desires. We eventually learned to accept each other and to respect each other's freedom. When we communicated in a healthier way, our trust grew and our walls came down. At these times our communication became a means of building unity rather than a catalyst for increasing division.

I wish I could say we had mastered healthy communication after forty-two years of marriage. But that would not be true. Even during the best of times, our communication was not perfectly life-giving and unifying. And, in contrast, even in the worst of times, aspects of our communication allowed us to hear and care for each other. I believe this is true in some way for all married couples, including you and your spouse. Let's take a moment to explore how this plays out in your life and marriage.

Take a Moment

1. Imagine yourself in the demonstration as Adam and Eve with the Trinity. What do you experience as you embrace each other while surrounded by the love of the Trinity?

2. What happens to trust when we try to have unity without devoting ourselves to each other through covenant?

3. In your experience, how do dishonor and coercion impact unity? What forms of communication foster lasting communion?

Five Key Areas

As we have noted, communion develops through healthy communication. But not all communication is equally impacting. I have discovered that there are five key areas of communication that are essential for developing marital unity. These five key areas are spiritual unity, emotional intimacy, daily companionship, cooperative teamwork, and sexual fulfillment.

The following table highlights these five key areas of marital unity (left-hand column), showing the communication practices that are essential for cultivating unity in each area (center column) and the obstacles that stand in the way of healthy communication (right-hand column).

AREAS OF COMMUNION	MEANS OF COMMUNICATING	OBSTACLES TO COMMUNICATION
SPIRITUAL UNITY	Praying and Worshipping	Apathy and Opposition
EMOTIONAL INTIMACY	Listening and Expressing	Wounds and Unforgiveness
DAILY COMPANIONSHIP	Working and Recreating	Isolation and Selfishness
COOPERATIVE TEAMWORK	Mutual Submitting and Agreeing	Control and Self-Reliance
SEXUAL FULFILLMENT	Expressing Affection and Lovemaking	Lust and Lack of Desire

These five areas of unity, though distinct, are mutually interdependent. Together they express our devotion in marriage. Each one strengthens the others and builds on the previous one. They are listed in the order of progression. *Spiritual unity* is the foundation upon which the other four areas of unity are built. Everything in marriage depends on a solid spiritual foundation. This is only common sense, because without genuine love and faithfulness, everything falls apart. The sacraments, lived authentically, provide the basis for spiritual unity. As they are lived out in regular prayer and worship, couples can cultivate strong bonds of communion with God and each other. Conversely, apathy and spiritual opposition are primary obstacles to worship and prayer and thus hinder spiritual unity.

Building on the foundation of spiritual unity, the next key area is *emotional intimacy*. When love and respect permeate the relationship, couples naturally grow in trusting each other. In an atmosphere of emotional safety, they can express themselves openly with an overall sense of confidence that they will be listened to and received by their spouse. This in turn enhances greater intimacy. On the other hand, when there is any kind of betrayal in the relationship and wounds are left unhealed, or when unresolved issues in the relationship lead to a buildup of resentments and unforgiveness, emotional connection is hindered. These issues need to be addressed and resolved so that emotional connection can be restored.

When spiritual unity and emotional intimacy are present, couples naturally gravitate toward wanting to spend time together. This is the third key area of marital communion: *daily companionship.* Whether working side by side or enjoying a favorite recreational activity together, companionship allows a couple to experience a sense of belonging that is one of the key features of marital unity. By contrast, isolation and selfish preoccupations weaken companionship. To overcome these obstacles, couples must dedicate themselves to finding time together to engage in enjoyable work and spend quality time in recreation activities. This is enhanced by establishing daily routines and rituals that build companionship.

As couples grow in the first three levels of communion, they are more readily able to establish *cooperative teamwork* in their marriage. Teamwork allows couples to be of "one mind and one heart" as they face the challenges and decisions in their common life together. Teamwork encompasses many important tasks such as decision-making, money management, parenting, time management, boundary setting, and so on. Those couples who put aside their pride and learn to submit to each other in love can find creative ways to make mutually satisfying decisions. When this occurs, they remain together on the same team. But when one or both stubbornly refuse to cooperate, decision-making becomes a battle for control, thus hindering the development of unity in teamwork.

Sexual fulfillment is the last of the five key areas of unity. When couples have a vibrant spiritual unity, are emotionally intimate, and have developed companionship and teamwork, their sexual relationship expresses the fulfillment of their overall sense of communion. Sexual fulfillment includes the whole range of activities from intimate expressions of affection to passionate lovemaking. Feeling deeply connected and mutually cherished, married couples can give themselves to each other, freely, fully, faithfully, and fruitfully. The main obstacles to sexual fulfillment are lust, which is an attitude of using each other for self-pleasure, and lack of desire, which often results from feeling used. Typically, these obstacles build on each other. When self-gratification is involved, lack of desire eventually follows.

These five areas of unity are mutually interdependent—when one area grows stronger it helps strengthen the other areas. Collectively, they are rooted in a strong covenant bond and are cultivated daily by honoring and honest communication. When these foundations are present in marriage, couples can navigate through the obstacles that threaten their intimacy in order to establish an ever-growing trust and unity. Throughout the rest of part I, we will be exploring these five areas in greater depth, focusing on one area in each chapter. In part II, in order to understand the source of conflicts and to bring about healing and reconciliation where this is needed, we will address how to face and overcome the obstacles that stand in the way of communion.

Before moving on to the next chapter to address the first of these areas (*spiritual unity*), I encourage you to take a moment to reflect on these five areas of unity in your relationship. If you are married or engaged, I strongly encourage you to complete the "State of Your Union Address" in the Activity for Couples. It will prepare you to receive the most benefit throughout the rest of the book.

Take a Moment

These can be answered individually, as a couple, or in a group discussion.

1. What are the five key areas of marital unity and why are they important for *your* marriage?

2. What communication skills are needed for each area? What is your weakest area? Strongest?

3. What are the key obstacles that prevent unity in each area? Which obstacle are you most aware of in your marriage?

Activity for Couples: State of Your Union Address

This is an opportunity to assess these five key areas of marital unity in your relationship. Write down your answers separately. Be honest with yourself. Then share a summary of each area with your spouse. As you share these assessments of your relationship, do so with mutual respect and honor, desiring to hear and understand what your spouse perceives in each area. This is not a time for arguing or coercing. Allow the communication on these areas of your relationship to build intimacy and understanding, which will eventually bring greater communion between you in the long run.

A. Spiritual Unity

1. How would you describe the spiritual unity in your marriage?
2. Describe how, when, and how often you pray and worship together.
3. What are the obstacles that interfere with your spiritual unity?
4. What changes do you desire in your spiritual relationship together?

B. Emotional Intimacy

1. On a scale of 1 to 10, rate the level of emotional intimacy in your marriage (1 being the lowest and 10 being the highest).
2. How well do you each express your emotions and listen to each other?
3. What are the barriers that interfere with your emotional intimacy?
4. What changes do you believe would help nurture emotional intimacy in your marriage?

C. Daily Companionship

1. What activities do you enjoy engaging in as a couple?

2. What are the daily rituals (work, leisure, other) that help you maintain companionship?

3. Do you feel that your needs for companionship are being met? Why or why not?

4. What would improve your companionship? Are you willing to invest the time and energy to make this happen?

D. Cooperative Teamwork

1. Describe the overall level of cooperation and teamwork in your marriage.

2. In what areas do you need to improve your teamwork and cooperation?

3. In what areas of your marriage are you experiencing a battle of wills?

4. How do you feel about practicing mutual submission in your marriage? Are you willing to practice it? Why or why not?

E. Sexual Fulfillment

1. Is your sexual relationship mutually fulfilling? Explain.

2. Do you give yourself freely and fully to each other in your sexual embrace? When and how do you withhold affection and sexual intimacy with each other?

3. Are you both faithful to your marriage and open to offspring? Where is lust, objectification, self-pleasuring, or lack of interest a problem in your sexual fulfillment?

4. What changes would you like to see in this area that would bring you both greater fulfillment?

3

ROOTED IN CHRIST: SPIRITUAL UNITY

*Unless the LORD build the house, they labor
in vain who build.*
—Psalm 127:1

At the end of the last chapter, I encouraged you to assess your spiritual unity as a couple as part of your personal State of Your Union Address. You were asked to describe how and when you pray and worship together as a couple, the obstacles that frustrate your spiritual unity, and the changes you would like to see in order to strengthen this most important area of your relationship. If you haven't completed this activity yet, I encourage you to go back and conduct the reflection before beginning this chapter. Answering these questions will help you personalize everything we discuss in this chapter in order to strengthen this foundational part of your marriage.

When I look back over my marriage with Margie, I recognize that early on I thought we were compatible in our faith background and spirituality. Later, our lack of spiritual unity almost destroyed our marriage. Yet in the most difficult season of our marriage, I was awakened from my apathy and discovered an underlying foundation of faith that held us together in the face of a ferocious spiritual opposition. At the end of our marriage, we saw the fruits of all that God had done throughout the years in answering our prayers.

When we were first married, I mistakenly thought we had a solid spiritual unity. Having been raised Catholic, we both went to Mass weekly and attended Catholic grade school and high school. We chose to be married in the Church and entered our sacrament with good intentions. These outward signs of faith led me to conclude that we had a solid spiritual foundation and the basis for unity in our marriage. But what I didn't realize is that we had a lot of cracks in our spiritual foundation.

We both called ourselves Christians, but some of the most important choices we made before marriage weren't in accordance with Christ's teaching. When it came time to make those decisions, we didn't turn to the Holy Spirit for guidance. In fact, in a few of those important decisions, we did exactly the opposite: we turned away from what we knew to be God's will and did want we wanted instead. One example came with our sexual relationship before marriage. We both knew that engaging in sexual intimacy before marriage was a direct violation of God's holy will, but we did it anyway. Though my conscience bothered me, I justified it in my mind, saying to myself, *We are going to marry each other eventually, so what's the big deal?* We also began using contraception before marriage. I rationalized this away by saying I couldn't find the Church's teaching about contraception anywhere in scripture. I shudder now realizing I used God's Word to resist his will and to justify our sin. To make matters worse, neither of us confessed these sins before we entered into marriage.

Later, after giving birth to our second daughter, Margie decided she wanted to have a tubal ligation. Though I desired more children and was not supportive of the idea, I consented to her decision. (I thought I was respecting her freedom, because it was her body.) All of this occurred before we reached the five-year mark of our marriage. These choices created big cracks in our spiritual foundation. Though neither of us seemed to be aware of the breach at the time, I later realized these decisions cut us off from a vital relationship with the Holy Spirit.

In retrospect, the effects of our choices became evident in our daily interactions. During those first years of our relationship, we never thought of praying together or going to Confession, and we only attended Mass occasionally. We allowed resentments to build up between us. When we tried to address them, we failed to approach each other with humility. In the heat of our conflicts, we neglected to love and cherish each other with our thoughts and words, though we had promised each other on the day of our wedding that we would. We both professed belief in God, but some of our actions and decisions told a different story.

In my late twenties, I experienced the beginning of a spiritual awakening that I described in chapter 1. I finally understood that my lack of devotion to God was also affecting my relationship with Margie. In response, I began praying and reading scripture regularly. The Holy Spirit then led me to face those areas of unconfessed sins from earlier in our relationship by helping me realize it was spiritual rebellion to choose my will over God's. Simultaneously, the Holy Spirit also began to reveal my childhood wounds that I had kept buried for many years.

I deeply desired Margie to share in this spiritual renewal with me, but she resisted for many years. My renewed spiritual enthusiasm ended up creating a greater division between us, emotionally and spiritually. By the time we were in our early thirties, this crack in the foundation of our relationship became a huge crevice. Our lack of spiritual unity was a key factor in tempting us to divorce. This core division was deeply painful for both of us, and neither one of us could see how we could go on together with this chasm between us.

But thank God, when things came to a head, we finally talked about our feelings openly. After acknowledging my emotional bankruptcy, I said to Margie, "I feel the only option is to divorce, but I can't believe it is God's will." Her response startled me. She stated simply, "It isn't." In that moment, my eyes were opened, and I could see she still valued our sacrament and cared about doing God's will. With both of us recognizing our marriage as a sacrament of Christ's love, I realized we had a spiritual foundation to build upon together.

The Sacrament of Matrimony

Sacraments are Jesus' life-giving words, practically lived, in the power of the Holy Spirit. When practiced authentically, sacraments have the potential to transform every area of our lives. But few of us appreciate this reality fully. Many of us tend to look at sacraments as antiquated rituals that have no bearing on our lives in the present. We aren't aware of the powerful spiritual dynamism that remains present within each sacrament, at every moment of our lives.

That was certainly true for Margie and me early in our marriage. We looked at our sacrament as something that occurred in the past rather than what it truly was—the grace to love each other each moment of our lives together. Like many others who are married in the Church, we had spiritual amnesia. We professed our vows to each other, but then failed to act on them in our daily actions. We didn't depend on the power of the Holy Spirit to love each other freely, fully, faithfully, and fruitfully, though we had promised to do that on our wedding day.

In my work as a therapist, I saw that Margie and I were not the only ones who failed to live our sacrament authentically. Most of the Christian couples I counseled during my years as a marriage therapist seemed to suffer from the same disconnect between the sacred vows they professed and the way they interacted with each other in daily life. Like Margie and me, they didn't see the relevance of their sacrament in the way they related to each other, including how they faced conflicts, made decisions, engaged in lovemaking, and prayed together as a couple. I could understand, because we too lived that way for many years in our marriage.

This lackadaisical attitude many of us have regarding the Sacrament of Matrimony stands in stark contrast with the Church's beautiful vision for marriage. Notice the enthusiasm of Tertullian, who lived a few centuries after Jesus, as he speaks of the purpose and dignity of a marriage that is blessed by the Church: "How can I ever express the happiness of the marriage that is joined together by the Church, strengthened by an offering, sealed by a blessing, announced by angels and ratified by the Father? . . . How wonderful the bond between two believers with a single hope, a single desire, a single observance, a single service! They are both brethren and both fellow-servants; there is no separation between them in spirit or flesh; in fact, they are truly two in one flesh and where the flesh is one, one is the spirit."[1]

Tertullian affirms what the Church has always taught about Holy Matrimony. First and foremost, it is a holy bond mirroring our union with Christ. Look at all the ways Tertullian emphasizes the bond of unity that is created through the sacrament: "How wonderful the bond between two believers." "There is no separation between them." They have become "two in one flesh." They are one in the Spirit. Do you hear his emphasis on *spiritual unity*? This is your inheritance. If you have been "joined together by the Church," you *already* have been given the gift of spiritual unity in your marriage. No matter how connected or disconnected you may feel with your spouse on any given day, you are united to each other in ways beyond your ability to fully comprehend. This, as St. Paul says so eloquently, is a *great mystery* (see Eph 5:32).

In God's eyes, if you are living in a state of grace, *your marriage is holy*. Do you realize that? This is the key to having a good marriage—seeing your relationship the way God sees it and allowing Jesus' self-giving love to be expressed through you. By yielding to the promptings of the Holy Spirit, you come to discover that spiritual unity has been there all along. When you fail to live this way, don't give up, the Sacrament of Reconciliation is available to restore you in holiness, and the Eucharist is an ongoing source of grace and strength.

For many of us, this is a radical departure from the way we see our marriage relationship amid all the seemingly mundane rituals and routines of marriage. We need the eyes of faith to see this deeper reality. Remember the demonstration I described in the last chapter, of Adam and Eve embracing each other in the protective cocoon of the Father, Son, and Holy Spirit. That is a good visual representation of spiritual unity in marriage.

God designed marriage to be experienced in this way, as a communion with the Holy Trinity. When you allow yourselves and your relationship to be immersed in God's all-encompassing love, you remain connected with him and with each other. When you leave that protective covering of God's love and wander off on your own, you put yourselves and your marriage in jeopardy. In hindsight, I see that Margie and I put our marriage in jeopardy from the very beginning by not establishing our foundation in the Lord. For many years we were blinded to the effects of our choices. How about you? Take a moment for reflection on spiritual unity in your marriage.

Take a Moment

1. Do you believe spiritual unity is essential for a good marriage? Why or why not?

2. When you read Tertullian's description of the Sacrament of Matrimony, how does that compare with your view of marriage?

3. Do you express your spiritual unity by worshipping and praying together as a couple? Explain.

Worshipping God Together

Most of us are familiar with the phrase "Families that pray together stay together." This modern proverb has been validated by scholarly research and reaffirmed repeatedly by the faithful witness of many couples who make worship and prayer a priority in their marriage. According to research studies, married couples who regularly pray and worship with each other are generally happier than those who don't. In fact, couples who pray together daily and formally worship together at least weekly have the highest likelihood of staying married for life. They also experience a greater appreciation of their spiritual unity while seeing the fruits of their prayers and worship permeate all the other areas of their relationship.[2]

Do you and your spouse regularly pray and worship together like this? If not, I strongly encourage you to do so. In addition to expressing your devotion to God, it is the best insurance you can provide for your marriage and family. That's because authentic prayer and worship honors God as the true center of your lives and relationship, ahead of every other attachment. Putting God first protects you from idolizing your marriage or looking to your spouse to satisfy all your needs. Furthermore, adoring God and depending on him is the only way to integrate every aspect of your life. Authentic worship is the foundation of spiritual unity (see *CCC* 2114).

Worship heals us by awakening our hearts to the passionate love and generosity of God. As we actively engage in thanking him, we learn to see everything, including our marriage, as a gift of his loving-kindness for us. This is expressed beautifully by Ann Voskamp in her bestselling book *One Thousand Gifts*: "Giving thanks awakens me to a God giving Himself, the naked, unashamed passion, God giving himself *to me.*"[3] This awakening in turn motivates us to respond in kind, desiring to give ourselves freely and fully while maintaining heartfelt gratitude for all the ways God and our spouse give to us generously.

Worshipping in this way frees us from self-centeredness. Slowly, we are transformed in Christ, to love as he loves. In his book *Spousal Love*, Deacon James Keating describes how married couples are taken up into Christ's self-offering in worship: "Worshipping at Mass is the highest form of prayer since during this worship we are taken up into Christ's own self-offering, to the Father out of love for His Bride, the Church. . . . We can't even understand what marriage is unless we look at how Christ loves the Church, till the end (Jn 13:1)."[4]

Worshipping together at Mass with this level of awareness means bringing every aspect of our marriage into Christ's self-offering. During the penitential rite, we are invited to name and release specific faults born of selfishness so we can love more freely. During the Liturgy of the Word, as we attentively listen to God speak to our hearts, his wisdom inspires us to love more faithfully. At the offertory, as we give thanks to the Father for all his generous gifts, we can offer ourselves fully, in union with Christ's self-offering. At the consecration, in the silence of our hearts, we can renew our baptismal vows to Jesus (as Bridegroom) as well as our marriage vows, remembering that our life and marriage have been consecrated to Christ. At the end of the Eucharistic Prayer, we reaffirm with our *Amen* that our marriage is to be lived daily "through him, with him, and in him." In praying the Our Father and exchanging the sign of peace, we pray for God's will to be done in every aspect of our lives, including our marriage. We also forgive anyone, including our spouse, for whatever might hinder our communion with Jesus.

As we receive the Precious Body and Blood of Christ in Holy Communion, we pray for greater communion with each other. Deacon Keating encourages married couples to ask for special graces during this time after receiving Communion: "Couples should let Jesus live His spousal love for the Church over again in their own love for one another. They do this by simply asking Him in prayer to do so, and by sharing their needs and desires with Him: 'Lord, live your spousal love for the Church over again in me. Help me to love my spouse like you love the Church. Love my spouse for me and with me.'"[5]

Can you see how worshipping in this way can transform your marriage? Obviously, this kind of worship and prayer is not just reserved for Mass. Authentic worship must permeate all the little moments of our daily life as a couple and family, including the ways we interact with each other, our children, and those outside our home. Too many of us know the experience of fighting on the way to Mass and forgetting Jesus as soon as we leave Mass. Keating warns that if Jesus is not spoken about outside of Sunday Mass, something dangerous happens: "We begin to think that God is not accessible in the ordinariness of our days."[6] Voskamp adds, "The Communion service is only complete *in service*. Communion, by necessity, always leads us into community."[7]

This is the ultimate purpose of your marriage: to live in communion with Christ and with each other so your children and many others will know they were destined for love. Communion is always possible, because Jesus promised he would remain with us (see Mt 28:20). Yet we can be oblivious to his presence if we are not devoted in prayer. Prayer is the second main communication practice, along with worship, that fosters spiritual unity. In prayer, we draw upon the multifold graces of the sacraments in our daily lives.

Daily Prayer

Prayer is like breathing. We need to breathe at every moment to stay alive. Similarly, we need to pray unceasingly to keep love and trust alive in marriage and to continue to grow in our spiritual unity as a couple. Along with worship, prayer is the most important communication that takes place in your marriage, because it shapes every other aspect of your relationship. Every decision you make in your marriage is an opportunity to ask the Holy Spirit for guidance. Every time you engage in lovemaking or enter into an intimate conversation, if you incorporate prayer, you cultivate the fruit of the Spirit (love, joy, peace, patience, kindness, goodness, faithfulness, generosity, and self-control). Who wouldn't want a relationship filled with these abundant fruits of love?

Praying together as a couple also invokes blessings upon your marriage (and family) in ways you can't even imagine. When you pray together on a regular basis, you become more docile to the Holy Spirit, which then affects all the ways you love and serve each other. Every time you spend time together in work or recreation, you can become aware that Jesus remains with you, strengthening your bond of companionship. When you suffer times of loneliness in your marriage, like we all do, prayer allows you to know that you are never alone, because Jesus is intimate with you. When you fail to love and cherish each other, prayer allows you to receive God's forgiveness and then humbly ask for your spouse's forgiveness.

You would think this awareness of these essential benefits of prayer would be enough motivation for couples to be dedicated to praying together often, but I have found that many couples have difficulty making prayer a priority. Though there are many reasons for this, I believe there are two primary obstacles that interfere with worshipping and praying together in marriage. These are *apathy* and *spiritual opposition*.

Apathy and Spiritual Opposition

Apathy seeps into a relationship when passion and devotion are missing. It is an expression of the sin of sloth and the primary obstacle most couples face when it comes to praying and worshipping together. Remember my experience in the Bible study when Jesus spoke to me about "being lukewarm" (Rv 3:17)? It awakened me to the realization that I had been apathetic in my relationship with him for many years. Most of the time I didn't even have the desire to pray or worship. Even when I did pray or attend worship, I often did so half-heartedly, without much heartfelt passion.

Since then, I have discovered that I was not the only one to suffer from this spiritual malaise. Many Christian marriages suffer from apathy in their spiritual unity, especially when it comes to worship and prayer. Most couples seem to have little time for prayer or interest in worship, either together or on their own.

Have you ever stopped to consider the grave injustice to God due to our spiritual apathy? During Mass, we celebrate Jesus' *Passion*, where he pours himself out to us as our Bridegroom, wholeheartedly and with the greatest possible generosity. He holds nothing back. Yet, too often, we worship him with little to no passion and barely give ourselves in response. Lacking heartfelt enthusiasm, we can seem more dead than alive when we engage in prayer or worship activities. Can you imagine your spouse making love with you and exuding the same level of passion that we often express in worshipping our divine Bridegroom? Would you feel loved and desired? I shudder to think of how Jesus feels due to our spiritual apathy when he gives so fully.

Apathy not only weakens our devotion; it also makes us vulnerable to spiritual opposition. I never gave much thought to spiritual battle until things became desperate during the winter season of my marriage. More than anything else, that struggle opened my eyes to the influence of hostile spiritual forces actively opposing our marriage. It was almost too late before I realized that the "father of lies" was intentionally trying to destroy our marriage by creating a division between Margie and me while tempting us to deny our sacred vows.

At the time, I was largely unaware of the deceiver's influence. But after we made it through that crisis, the Holy Spirit began to show me the tremendous spiritual battle that was going on for my soul, and for our marriage.

Through prayer and spiritual reading, I came to realize that there were many different points of access that made me and our marriage vulnerable to intense spiritual attack during this time.[8] Our unhealed wounds and unconfessed sins were the most glaring access points. But there were others as well, including the generational influences from my parents' divorce, and the spiritual atmosphere in our house, even before we moved in. We never thought of having our house blessed, even though the couple who owned the house before us divorced, unwittingly inviting unholy spirits of division and divorce into the house.

Each of these areas of access made us vulnerable to spiritual opposition. After seeing for myself the reality of demonic influences, I began to understand why the Church encourages us to get our house blessed and urges us to be fervent in prayer: "Such a battle and such a victory become possible only through prayer" (*CCC* 2849).

After working through our marital struggles, and with the insights that came afterward, I realized prayer was not something I could afford to be apathetic about. For the sake of my spiritual well-being, our marriage, and all the members of our family, as well as for the larger Church community, I needed to be devoted to God and to make prayer and worship the center of my life and the cornerstone of our marriage.

As the Spirit led me over the years, I grew in my desire and dedication to pray and worship daily. Every morning, as I knelt before an image of Jesus' Sacred Heart, I asked God to continue to heal each of our hearts and our marriage. I also prayed that he would protect us from evil (which separates and divides) and bring us into communion with him and with each other. Month after month, year after year, as I continued to pray this way, God led me through a process of personal transformation and gave us the grace of perseverance.

The changes in me and our marriage were imperceptible at times. I was often tempted to give up when Margie and I did not seem to be making the kind of progress I desired in our spiritual unity. But as he often does, God saved his best for last, just like at the wedding of Cana, when the latter wine was better than the first (see Jn 2:9–10). When Margie got sick, I could finally see the fruit of those prayers that I had been praying for the past thirty years of our married life. God filled us with a new outpouring of his love and grace.

Margie had resisted praying together for much of our married life, aside from grace at meals. But over the last several months of Margie's life, we prayed together multiple times each day, starting in the morning and ending when we went to bed at night. In the mornings, when I returned from daily Mass, I brought the Eucharist home to Margie. We first prayed an Our Father together. At times, our children and grandchildren joined us during this beautiful experience of Holy Communion. Through it all, God showed me that he had been listening to our prayers throughout the years, and that he had never left us.

I write all this to encourage you, no matter where you are in your spiritual unity as a couple. If your marriage has been consecrated to Christ, you are already united in the Spirit because of your sacrament. If your marriage or home has not been blessed, I encourage you to do so as quickly as possible. And begin to pray immediately for your marriage.

Whether or not your spouse desires to pray with you, you can still pray for your relationship. In approaching your spouse, I encourage you to proceed gently and invite him or her without coercion or pressure. Early on I made the mistake of thinking I could convince Margie to pray and worship with me before she was ready. Worship and prayer are very intimate experiences and must be engaged in freely. So approach *praying together* with great reverence and respect for each other.

Praying Together

Even when we realize the necessity of praying together as a couple, many of us are unsure how to go about it. We may have insecurities and anxieties about praying out loud. We may not even know what to say or how to say it. We may even wonder if our prayers are being heard. But it is relieving to know we don't have to rely on ourselves to learn how to pray. The scriptures assure us that the Holy Spirit lives in us and is already interceding for us in our weaknesses (Rom 8:26). Jesus himself is also praying for us (Jn 17; Rom 8:34). We can be assured he is praying for our spiritual unity, because this was the focus of his personal prayer for all of us in the Upper Room before his Crucifixion: "I pray . . . that *they may be one . . . as we are one* . . . [so] they may be *brought to perfection as one*" (Jn 17:20–23, emphasis added).

Jesus' prayer reveals his yearning, as our Bridegroom, for spiritual unity with us. It also reveals his desire and intention for our spiritual unity with one another. He won't stop praying until this intention is fully realized. He desires our spiritual unity so we can be deeply fulfilled and become a vibrant witness of his love to everyone around us. He invites us to pray with him for these same intentions. Trust that your prayers will be heard, because the Father desires their fulfillment even more than you do.

When we are unsure about how to pray, Jesus will teach us, just as he did with the disciples before us (see Lk 11:1–13). He taught them a way of praying that has been passed down to every generation of believers. It has become the most common prayer of the Church: the Our Father. While we pray this individually and in community, I have come to realize that it is a particularly powerful prayer for married couples, because it confronts the varied obstacles that hinder unity in marriage and offers the antidote for each of these obstacles.

Too many of us rattle off this prayer with little thought. But Jesus never intended the Our Father to be a formula prayer, to be repeated mechanically.[9] Rather, it is the intimate conversation between us and our *heavenly Father*, asking for his grace, guidance, provision, healing, and protection. He is *always faithful* to respond. Recited with faith and with an open heart, this can be a powerful and healing prayer for your marriage. I can assure you that as you pray this prayer with heartfelt devotion, and faithfully practice these petitions in your marriage, the Father will transform every aspect of your relationship.

At the end of this chapter you will have an opportunity to pray the Our Father together (or individually) for your marriage. Before you do so, I invite you to meditate on the meaning of each petition and consider how each one applies to your marriage. The first phrase of the prayer invites you to address God intimately, as your heavenly Father. The rest of the petitions are ways to confidently call on his fatherly care for your daily needs as a couple and within your family, and for protection from the spiritual opposition that threatens to destroy your unity. Recite each petition slowly and with understanding:

> *Our Father*: You and your spouse are beloved children of the Father. He is your *Abba*. Take a moment and imagine you and your spouse resting on Jesus' heart together.

> *who art in heaven*: Heaven is where God dwells. As you pray together, realize that heaven is in your midst.

> *hallowed be thy name*: God is holy. Prayer brings us in touch with our desire as a married couple to grow in union with him and to release our impurities.

> *Thy kingdom come*: Invite his kingdom of "righteousness, peace, and joy in the Holy Spirit" (Rom 14:17) into your relationship.

> *thy will be done on earth, as it is in heaven*: Let go of your control and surrender your self-centered will to seek God's holy will.

Give us this day our daily bread: Ask the Father for whatever you need in your marriage and family today.

and forgive us our trespasses, as we forgive those who trespass against us: Let go of guilt, shame, and resentment, as you forgive each other from the heart.

and lead us not into temptation: Acknowledge your weaknesses and disordered desires and ask God to transform these desires into his holy desires, as you are strengthened to overcome temptations.

but deliver us from evil: Our victory over evil influences is not in our own strength but in Christ (see *CCC* 2854).

Having reflected on the petitions of the Our Father, practice praying together. It will only take a few minutes. The fruit will be well worth the investment. But first, I invite you to take a moment to reflect on the primary obstacles to prayer and worship and how to combat them.

Take a Moment

1. Are you devoted to praying together? Where do you recognize apathy and spiritual opposition in your prayer and worship, individually and as a couple?

2. Review the section about praying through the different parts of the Mass with a focus on your marriage. What are your thoughts about worshipping together in this way?

3. What stood out to you as you walked through the Our Father prayer?

Activity for Couples: Praying Together

1. Pray the Our Father together very slowly; entertain the meaning of each petition. If you are willing, hold hands during the prayer. Keep the focus on your marriage: Our Father . . . may your kingdom come (in our marriage), and may your will be done (in our lives) as it is in heaven. Give us our daily bread (be specific about what you need). Forgive us our trespasses as we forgive each other (actively forgive each other for any areas where you are holding on to resentments).

2. Worship is an expression of gratitude for all the good God has given us. After praying the Our Father, take turns offering a prayer of thanksgiving for your spouse out loud. The husband goes first: Heavenly Father, I thank you for the gift my wife is for me and our family. Thank you for . . . (name specific areas of gratitude). Then, the wife prays a prayer of thanksgiving for her husband.

3. Blessing is a way of invoking God's presence. Take turns blessing each other. (If you are both willing, place a hand on your spouse's shoulder.) The wife goes first: "Please bless (name) and fill him with your love, please give him (whatever you desire for your husband)." Then the husband blesses the wife.

4. When you receive Jesus in the Eucharist, pray for the needs of your spouse and for a greater ability and willingness to love with Jesus' self-giving love.

5. When you begin to experience conflict in your marriage, pray the Rosary together and renounce any unloving thoughts in prayer.

4

HEART TO HEART: EMOTIONAL INTIMACY

For no one hates his own flesh but rather
nourishes and cherishes it.
—Ephesians 5:29

Do you remember the intimate conversations you had with each other before you were married? I trust you had some, or else you probably wouldn't have fallen in love and decided to marry in the first place. When I think back to the beginning of my relationship with Margie, I'm led to the time before we were dating. We were good friends, without any romantic interest in each other at the time. It all started when Margie, a year older than me and a senior in high school, offered to drive me to school every day. She had a driver's license and a car. I had neither.

In the months that followed, driving back and forth to school together, our discussions spanned many areas of our lives as we got to know each other intimately. We felt comfortable and at ease in each other's presence. We would speak freely and personally with each other. Over time our friendship grew, and with it our love and respect for each other, though I never imagined that these conversations would lead us to marriage one day. The day of her graduation from high school is when I realized my feelings for Margie went beyond friendship. As I said goodbye to her at graduation, I couldn't bear the thought of never seeing her again. The next day at a graduation party, we both realized how much we had grown to love each other. Within three weeks, I knew she was the one with whom I wanted to spend the rest of my life. That certainty came about through hours of intimate conversations, night after night, sitting on the front steps of her house. Time seemed to fly by. After hours of talking, we would reluctantly say goodnight around midnight (her curfew), only to start over again the next evening. I marvel that during that season we never ran out of things to share with each other. It was the springtime of our love, with all the beauty and sweetness that comes with the blossoming of emotional intimacy.

There is nothing like that feeling of falling in love and feeling deeply connected to your beloved. Trusting you will be received and cherished, you can share almost anything and everything. Those conversations are often deeply nourishing to our respective souls. They add to our feelings of security in the relationship and fill us with unspeakable joy. Thinking back to that time in our relationship, I smile with gratitude and remember the passionate attraction we felt. We wanted to express our love with our entire beings, body and soul.

In the later years of marriage, there can be a similar kind of connection, and oftentimes even deeper. We may miss the intensity of youthful passion, and the joy of discovering new things about each other. But in its place, we have a deep knowing and appreciation of all the days we spent together and all the ways that our lives have become intertwined. Reconciling after a painful time of disconnection, the intimacy can be even greater. The latter wine (of mature love) can be even sweeter than the first wine of falling in love. Mature intimacy is aged and seasoned by all the history that has been shared together as a couple over the years. With a mature intimacy, communication can occur without many words.

Nonverbal Intimacy

An experience with Margie a few weeks before she died stands out in my memory as one of those intimate conversations without many words. When Margie woke up on this particular morning, she could no longer speak coherently. Somehow overnight she had lost her capacity to articulate her thoughts. As much as I tried to listen attentively to what she was trying to say, I couldn't decipher her garbled words. I felt a sense of panic rising within me, realizing she would not be able to tell me what she needed and I wouldn't be able to help her. Just as quickly, my panic turned into feelings of deep grief, anticipating the loss of emotional connection that this would surely bring.

As these anxious thoughts and feelings flashed through my mind, I was still straining to make sense of what Margie was trying to articulate. But then my heart calmed, as she looked at me lovingly and managed to form a few coherent words: "I really appreciate your caring for me." (Just writing this now brings me to tears again.) Those few words turned out to be the last ones I would hear Margie speak. After that, she completely lost her capacity to express herself verbally. I became deeply grieved—for both of us and for our family.

In those moments of realization, my grief turned into remorse over all the wasted years of disconnection, when we hadn't nourished and cherished each other as well as we could have. I thought of the many occasions when we had the capacity to communicate with each other, but instead squandered the opportunity. I recounted the thousands of little moments we had wasted while arguing, being distant, not listening carefully, or not really attending to each other's needs or feelings. Now it was too late to get any of those moments back. Sometimes we don't cherish someone enough until we lose our ability to connect with them.

Later that morning, while praying, I sensed the Holy Spirit speaking to my heart, saying, "You can still communicate through your gaze and touch." Though comforted by the thought, I continued to feel intense sorrow over the loss of our emotional connection. I was also concerned as I contemplated how helpless and lonely Margie would feel with her inability to express her needs.

That same afternoon, my sister Kathy, who worked with Margie as a labor and delivery nurse for over twenty years, called to check on us. I shared with her what had happened that morning and my sorrow over Margie losing her ability to speak. Without me telling her what I had received in prayer that morning, Kathy confirmed the message. Speaking from her experience as a nurse, she assured me we could still communicate through our touch and gaze. With her confirmation, I knew God was speaking directly to my heart and encouraging me to continue to trust his presence and to love Margie as well as I could in this challenging situation.

Kathy's words of encouragement proved to be a tremendous consolation to me in my time of desolation. I was amazed by how much love and emotional connection Margie and I experienced in those remaining weeks, without her having the ability to express herself verbally. In some ways, the emotional connection was even more profound.

Connecting Emotionally

Have you noticed that when you feel emotionally connected to your spouse, everything else in life looks brighter and feels lighter? You face your day with an added bounce to your step. You feel more alive and joyful. When you are loved and cherished in this way, you also have a greater desire to nurture your partner. As trust grows, you feel more secure and are thus able to express your needs with greater openness and vulnerability. When you know your spouse is listening attentively and is attuned to you emotionally, you are more inclined to share your intimate thoughts, feelings, and desires with them, trusting that you will be received with kindness and compassion. During these times of emotional intimacy, communication flows spontaneously between you. You enjoy being in each other's company and miss each other when you are separated for any reason.

Wouldn't it be great if marriage was like this all the time? According to Dr. Gregory Popcak, a small number of married couples experience this level of intimacy most of the time. In these *exceptional 7 percent* of married couples, husbands and wives maintain a high level of emotional empathy. Despite the daily challenges of life, they remain emotionally connected as they honor and nurture each other consistently. They are well equipped to resolve conflicts and forgive hurts quickly, without allowing resentments to build up and create a distance between them. Conscious of their spouse's unique ways of giving and receiving love, they can listen well and minister to each other's needs. Overall, these couples maintain a high level of intimacy on a day-to-day basis and throughout all the years of their marriage.[1]

If this describes your marriage, consider yourself exceedingly blessed. Research has shown that husbands and wives who experience a high level of emotional connection with each other are psychologically, physically, and spiritually healthier than those who don't. That's because joy and happiness are the best medicine for our bodies and souls (see Prv 17:22, Neh 8:10). When we feel nurtured by our spouse, our hearts remain open and our connection with God and others is enhanced. We have more capacity to give love to everyone we know. Moreover, couples who are emotionally connected experience greater fidelity, stability, and satisfaction within their marriage. They also demonstrate an increased desire and energy for companionship and sexual intimacy, which creates a climate for cultivating trust and openness. These benefits extend to their entire family.[2]

Isn't this the kind of relationship we all desire in marriage? But not everyone experiences this joyful side of marriage on a regular basis. Many of us must overcome significant barriers that hinder our capacity for emotional intimacy.

Barriers to Emotional Intimacy

Regrettably, many married couples struggle when it comes to sustaining high levels of emotional intimacy. Unhealed emotional wounds and resentments (from past and present hurts) create barriers that make it difficult to trust and be vulnerable with each other. Some couples endure years of marriage like this, with little or no emotional connection to nourish them. Others taste emotional connection occasionally but find it hard to sustain over time. After fruitless attempts, some settle for a comfortable distance and resign themselves to a mediocre coexistence.

If your marriage fits this description, where there is little or no emotional intimacy, I sympathize with you, because a lack of nurturance in marriage can be chronically painful and mind-numbing. It is also bad for your physical, emotional, and spiritual health. Margie and I experienced emotional disconnection at various times throughout our marriage, and I have heard firsthand from many couples in therapy about the intense loneliness that comes from prolonged periods of emotional disconnection.

When emotional intimacy is missing in marriage, everything else is negatively affected. The consequences can be severe. Studies have found that over time, a consistent lack of emotional closeness is correlated with marital dissatisfaction; higher rates of anxiety and depression; a much greater risk of addiction, infidelity, and divorce; and a significant increase in physical and psychological illnesses.[3] These consequences are not only devastating to the married couple themselves but to their children and extended families as well.

If this is the reality in your marriage, you may be tempted to give up, like I was when Margie and I went through our most difficult season of disconnection. I understand how challenging this can be and feel compassion for both of you. At the same time, I want to encourage you to stay the course. It is well worth it. Things can and do change when you dedicate yourself to growing in your capacity to love, without demanding an immediate return. This is the nature of the true love you promised each other in the beginning. Genuine love "bears all things, believes all things, hopes all things, endures all things. Love never fails" (1 Cor 13:7–8). Remain faithful to your vows and continue to pray, asking God to heal your marriage. I can attest, from my own experience and in accompanying hundreds of married couples in their healing process over the years, that genuine love "never fails." In fact, it is the only thing that brings about transformation in our lives personally and within marriage.

I have witnessed many couples who had been stuck in chronic disconnection discover a beautiful new intimacy between them. I can't count the number of married couples who told me after months and sometimes years of therapy, "I could never imagine that we could love each other like this and feel so close after all those years of feeling so alone."

Many of these same couples reported that they had once felt close for a season early in their relationship (dating, courtship, and early marriage), but sooner or later they began drifting apart. Running up against seemingly impenetrable barriers to intimacy, they would eventually shut down emotionally with each other. Some continued to endure faithfully, while others turned their focus away from their marriage to find their fulfillment in work, children, recreation, or religious activities. A number found spousal substitutes in emotional or sexual infidelity. Others numbed the pain with addictions, such as food, alcohol, drugs, or pornography. (All these ways of coping are violations of the promise to be faithful.) As a result, the original hurt and loneliness became compounded exponentially.

Most of these couples didn't fully realize what was happening. Without knowing how they got there, they found themselves in a state of emotional desolation. But once we began exploring their marital dynamics in therapy, the issues came clearly into focus. A consistent pattern emerged. Each of these couples brought in unresolved emotional wounds and unconfessed areas of sin from their past. These inevitably carried over into their current relationship. When conflicts arose between them, their unresolved hurts created defensive barriers that blocked their ability to communicate effectively. Most of these couples were not aware of the source of their wounds. Moreover, they remained blinded to the deeper roots of bitterness that had hardened their hearts in unforgiveness, defiling their spouse and many others around them (see Heb 12:15).

After unsuccessful attempts to resolve the issues directly with their spouse, they often became frustrated and angry when their pain wasn't soothed or understood. They blamed their spouse for their suffering and demanded (implicitly or explicitly) that their spouse change to meet their needs. These tactics rarely resulted in increased emotional intimacy. Instead, they created more disconnection and resulted in even more negative judgments about each other's character.

As these negative thoughts and feelings colored their overall perceptions of their spouse, they lost hope (and desire) for intimacy. Frequently, further communication attempts would be met with defensive responses. Both partners eventually withdrew their hearts in self-protection. I understood these dynamics well because of my own experience in marriage. According to Dr. John Gottman, these patterns are present to some degree in every marriage relationship, but they become predominant in troubled marriages.[4] Do you recognize this pattern in your marriage in any way?

If this kind of marital dance is familiar to you, it doesn't mean you have a terminally bad marriage or that your marriage is hopeless. Perhaps your marriage is somewhere in the middle between the two extremes (of deep emotional connection and emotional divorce). Most couples have times of good emotional connection and times of isolation and loneliness where intimacy is lacking. Let's take a moment to reflect on how you experience emotional intimacy in your relationship.

Take a Moment

1. Describe an experience in your dating or marriage where you felt nourished and cherished. What contributed to the closeness you felt?

2. What barriers have gotten in the way of your emotional intimacy with your spouse?

3. How has emotional intimacy ebbed and flowed over the months and years of your marriage?

Seasons of Marriage

Recently, as I have been reflecting on my relationship with Margie, Gary Chapman's *The 4 Seasons of Marriage* has helped me gain a better understanding of these different seasons of connection and disconnection throughout our marriage. The book provides insight into the ebb and flow of emotional intimacy throughout the life cycle of most marriages.

There is a season for everything: "A time to plant, and a time to uproot the plant . . . a time to tear down, and a time to build . . . a time to weep, and a time to laugh" (Eccl 3:2–4). In nature, both planting and uprooting are essential for hearty growth. Chapman contends that marriages go through different seasons as well, from the "unsettledness of fall or the alienation and coldness of winter, toward the hopefulness of spring or the warmth and closeness of summer."[5]

While we experience these seasons of marriage very differently, they all have a time and a purpose. The spring and summer of our relationships are times for planting, building up, and joyful reaping. During these seasons, couples thrive with a high level of emotional connection. In contrast, the fall and winter seasons of marriage are often marked by times of uprooting, tearing down, and weeping over our barrenness. We experience less emotional connection to our spouse during these dark and chilly seasons. But sometimes God does his best work through these trying seasons of marriage.

I began reading *The 4 Seasons of Marriage* about six months after Margie passed away. Before starting it, I had been going through old letters and cards that Margie and I had written to each other over the years. We started writing letters when we were dating long distance, while I was away at college and Margie remained at home attending nursing school. We couldn't afford to call more than twice a week, so we found letters to be a good way to maintain our communication. (This was long before cell phones and emails were invented.) Even after we were married, we continued to write each other on special occasions. This was especially true during some of the difficult seasons of our marriage, when we were having trouble communicating with each other. We both learned that we could express ourselves better in writing.

As I reread the letters we had both written during our springtime of dating, I was reminded of how much we were in love and what it felt like to look to our future with hope. Conversely, the letters written during the most difficult and painful season of our marriage conveyed a very different outlook: We were both struggling to hold on to hope. During this wintry season, Margie and I were growing apart and feeling disconnected. We had a hard time hearing each other's needs because of our own pain and self-absorption.

Nearly every time we tried to communicate about our problems, we triggered each other's wounds again. Because neither of us enjoyed conflict, we each backed away when things became too intense. We would try again, only to run into the same barriers. It seemed the more we talked the worse things became. Resentments grew between us. We blamed and judged each other for our hurt. Though before and after this time we both had a strong commitment to our marriage, the temptation to divorce came often to our minds during this season as a way of escaping the helplessness and disconnect we felt. (Perhaps you can relate to a similar time in your marriage.)

During this fall/winter season, we reluctantly sought out marital therapy. But initially, therapy seemed to make things worse. We shared our hurt and unresolved anger with the therapist and each other, but it didn't help us connect emotionally. Neither of us could hear the other's suffering with compassion. We were too wrapped up in our own hurt and distorted perceptions. At one point, our therapist recommended that we separate, but neither of us wanted to do that. Instead, we tried writing letters to each other, attempting to share what we felt and what we needed. These were some of the letters I found around the time I received Chapman's book.

Rereading these letters in light of Chapman's descriptions of the four seasons of marriage opened my eyes in an entirely new way. I felt sad realizing how much I had misread Margie's intentions during that time. I could now sense her pain and feel her love in the letters in a way that I couldn't at the time they were written (thirty years earlier). I felt a new compassion for her, and for myself, as I saw and understood more clearly that we both needed to be loved, but each of us felt rejected and misunderstood instead. During these darkest wintry days, I seriously questioned my love for Margie and her love for me. But after reading these letters, I could see and feel how much I really loved her, and how much she truly loved me, despite our pain.

At the time these letters were written, I didn't realize that God was doing some of his best work in our hearts. But as I reread the letters again, I began to perceive the situation differently. I could see how God was uprooting the dead, bitter roots from our hearts, which had sprung up from our accumulated sins and wounds. Many of these bitter roots had been planted way before our marriage but were coming into effect in that season. I could finally see that this painful and lonely wintry season of our marriage had a *divine purpose*. We were being prepared for a new springtime of love that was still a few years away.

New Springtime

The uprooting and weeping of this difficult wintry season of our marriage eventually became the seeds of a new springtime of love between us. This winter season caused me to hunger for God, which in turn changed my heart toward Margie. When I called out to him in desperation, he answered my cry with a powerful, life-changing encounter with the Holy Spirit and a renewed vision for our marriage. My transformation occurred progressively over many months. As the springtime of our love became more evident, I felt a fresh love for Margie and was able to embrace her warmly and tenderly. This time, my weeping had a different quality. My tears were tears of joy, expressing gratitude for answered prayers and restored love. I came to really believe "that all things work for good for those who love God" (Rom 8:28), even in the fall and winter seasons of our marriages, when everything looks and feels barren.

My point in sharing this is to provide you with hope during any fall or winter seasons of your marriage, whether they are brief or extended periods. When you are in winter, feeling alone and desolate, remember that spring is coming. You may have to do some of the uprooting and tearing down first. There may also be some frozen places in the hearts of you and your spouse that need melting. But trust that the ice of winter can turn into the tears of spring, which will soften the soil of your hearts for a new springtime of love.

Without God, and without being devoted to each other in love, many couples falter during this trying time. Overwhelmed by loneliness and bitterness, they lose hope of having an emotional connection and instead distract themselves with the responsibilities of children or work. Some engage in affairs (emotional and sexual) or choose to divorce rather than walk through their pain and repent of their sins. Be on guard. It is far too easy during this painful season to harden your heart and conclude, like I did, that you are not in love anymore.

I urge you, when you face the fall and winter seasons in your marriage, big or small, to hold fast, pull up the bitter roots, and let your tears soften the ground of your hearts. If you are willing to do the hard work in this season, spring is surely coming, and with it a new hope and anticipation. During the springtime of love, you will let go of bitterness and judgments and learn new ways of nurturing and cherishing each other.

The way to emotional intimacy comes through learning how to listen attentively to your own emotions, as well as those of your spouse. This is critical, because your emotions are expressing the conditions of your hearts. In one way or another, they are echoes of love.

Echoes of Love

If you take the time to listen attentively to your intimate conversations, both good and bad, you can hear the echoes of love through all the desires and emotions you express to each other. This is the insight I received in rereading the letters Margie and I wrote to each other during our most difficult season.

According to St. Thomas Aquinas, all our "passions" are naturally ordered toward love.[6] Some emotions reveal the presence of love. Others reveal its absence. What we normally consider "positive" emotions are indicators that love is present. Conversely, the emotions we label as "negative" are revelations about the absence of love or threats to our security in being loved.

Think about how this applies in your marriage. Joy and happiness are natural expressions when you feel fulfilled in love; sorrow is what you feel anytime you experience loss of love. Peace is the natural emotional response when you feel securely loved; fear and anxiety arise when you feel insecure because love is threatened; anger is stirred when there is an injustice against love; compassion is awakened when you understand the pain underlying your own and your spouse's poor behavior. Hope is aroused when your desire for love seems possible; while despair and hopelessness settle in your heart when the possibility of love seems beyond your reach.

God created us with the capacity to experience the full range of these emotions. Every one of us can feel each emotion at any point in time, though some of us are more aware of what we feel and others less so. If you will stop to listen attentively to your emotions and to those of your spouse, they will reveal the condition of your hearts. They will also provide insight into the overall climate of your relationship and what season you may be in. Once you begin to recognize what's happening inside of you, you can become more attuned to your spouse's emotions. That will enable you to share your emotions constructively with your spouse and listen more compassionately to what he or she is experiencing regarding their needs being fulfilled.

In a healthy marriage, couples have built up enough trust with each other to enable them to express both positive and negative emotions with vulnerability and strength. They have the emotional freedom to express anger and gratitude, sorrow and joy. But they do so respectfully, in a way that honors their spouse and seeks communion of hearts. They can listen to each other and empathize with each other while maintaining healthy boundaries. They can likewise face conflict and grow from it.[7] In troubled marriages, by contrast, positive and negative emotions are either stifled and suppressed or expressed like a shotgun blasting anything in sight without regard to the damage. As couples engage in these destructive patterns of interacting, trust is diminished and healthy communication inevitably breaks down.[8]

For these reasons, St. James admonishes, "Everyone should be quick to hear, slow to speak, slow to wrath" (Jas 1:19). It is good to be aware when we are angry, but aggressively acting out our anger or passively avoiding it are symptoms of deeper unresolved issues in our hearts. Neither way of handling anger is conducive to building intimacy in marriage. When we yell and scream or withdraw our affections, we diminish trust and lose emotional connectedness. This can be counteracted by listening attentively to our loved one's needs and hurts, for behind most anger is unresolved hurt that needs to be expressed. When we share our inner experiences of hurt vulnerably without blame and condemnation, it aids mutual understanding and can facilitate healing.

When we don't deal with our pain constructively, we may too easily fall into depression or self-pity. Withdrawing physically and emotionally like a wounded animal retreating into the woods does little to bring about emotional closeness in marriage. Intimacy requires that we let our spouse know what is going on inside us. The word *intimacy* ("in-to-me-see") literally means "into fear." Intimacy usually involves some level of healthy risk and vulnerability. Conversely, when we don't constructively face our fears, we end up burying them or acting them out. One of the main ways we do this is by controlling those situations that are most threatening to us. We end up coercing our spouse rather than really communicating what is going on inside of us, like I did during the early parts of my marriage. This does little to build emotional intimacy or trust.

Sharing inner experiences vulnerably in an atmosphere of respect and trust is a way of being devoted to each other every day. It is the best way to cultivate emotional intimacy. From these intimate conversations, joy is the emotion that naturally emerges. Cultivating emotional intimacy is the way to plant the seeds of a joyful new springtime of love. The following reflection questions and couple exercises are designed to enhance your understanding of emotional intimacy as well as your capacity for sharing joy with each other.

Take a Moment

1. Which of the four seasons of marriage would you say you are currently in? What emotions are you feeling most during this season?

2. Which emotions do you have the greatest difficulty expressing to your spouse? What (internally and externally) makes it difficult to be vulnerable?

3. What could your spouse do to help you feel more emotionally secure?

Activity for Couples: Sharing Joy Stories

Take turns sharing an experience where you felt joy in the last twenty-four hours (due to an experience of love, accomplishment, or good news).

1. Directions for the wife: Share a "joy experience" with your husband—some situation or interaction that filled you with joy. Share your emotions with "I" statements with the goal of inviting your husband into an understanding of your experience so he can participate in your joy. Use feeling words to describe the experience. When you are finished sharing, and he responds, become the listener as he shares a joyful experience with you. (See directions for husband for how to listen.)

2. Directions for the husband: As you assume the role of listener, be attentive and attuned to your wife's feelings and facial expressions. Allow yourself to enter her joy emotionally. Remain quiet until she finishes her sharing; then reflect to her what you heard and saw in her expressions. After she is done sharing, share an experience of your own where you felt joy. (See directions for wife about how to share it.)

5

HAND IN HAND: DAILY COMPANIONSHIP

*It is not good for the man to be alone. I will
make a helper suited to him.*

—Genesis 2:18

Before Eve came along, Adam existed in a state of union with God, which St. John Paul II referred to as "original solitude."[1] But despite all the beauty and wonder of his intimacy with his Creator, something essential was still lacking in his experience of paradise. Adam was lonely for human relationship. He needed a suitable partner, a co-laborer in the garden, but more importantly, a *companion for his daily life*. Acknowledging this void, God remedied the situation by creating Eve. Coming from Adam's side, she would become the delight of his life, as evidenced by his exclamation: "This one, at last, is bone of my bones and flesh of my flesh" (Gn 2:23).

Adam's exuberant response greeting Eve for the first time has been echoed down through the centuries. Each of us shares in Adam's delight when we discover that special one who will be our lifelong companion. I remember vividly the excitement Margie and I shared as our wedding day approached, realizing that our time of separation (and long-distance relationship) would soon be over. We envisioned the simple day-to-day joys of being able to sleep together in the same bed, wake up in the same house, and share meals together at the same table every day. We could talk to each other any time we wanted, support each other in tough times, express affection freely any time we wanted, and sit side by side simply enjoying each other's company. We never had to be apart again (or so we thought).

Once married, we cherished this time with each other, but like many couples, when the newness of spending time together lost some of its luster, we began to take the gift of each other's company for granted. We didn't fully appreciate the immense blessing it was to have a "helpmate" accompany us through thick and thin, in sickness and in health, right up until the end.

At the end of Margie's life, I realized once again the tremendous gift that Margie's companionship had been throughout our marriage. And I consider it one of the greatest blessings of my life to have been able to accompany her through her final months, weeks, and hours on earth. In that final season of our marriage, God redeemed the lost moments of the past. He blessed us and our family with an intensely beautiful time of togetherness.

Separateness and Togetherness

Every married couple develops their own unique rhythm of sharing life together, which involves honoring their individual needs for solitude. Healthy companionship finds a good balance between establishing rituals and routines of togetherness while allowing each other the time and space to pursue separate interests and activities. This balance can fluctuate depending on the stages of married life and the needs of each person. Over the years, Margie and I experienced the satisfaction of companionship as well as the freedom to pursue our own interests. We also knew the loneliness of feeling disconnected and what it felt like to get out of balance and have too little companionship with each other. During those final weeks of Margie's life, we hardly left each other's side, day or night. Having our children, grandchildren, extended family, and close friends with us much of that time added to the sense of connectedness we felt. As Margie lost her ability to care for herself, our daughters, sons-in-law, and I joined forces to be by her side continuously. The amazing thing is that it was not burdensome to care for her or confining to be homebound. We all cherished the time we were able to spend together knowing that every moment was precious because of the impending separation.

With Margie's short-term memory loss due to her illness, she experienced life from one moment to the next. In many ways this "incapacity" gave us all a greater capacity to be present in the present moment. This ultimately added to our sense of connectedness. But it also had a downside, because Margie usually didn't remember what had happened fifteen minutes earlier. For example, when one of us would get up to get a drink of water or go to the bathroom, she would look at us wondering where we had gone (even though we just told her where we were going). When we came back into the room, her face lit up, and she would say, "Where were you? I missed you." It was sweet and sad at the same time. The sweetness came from the connection we felt. The sorrow from realizing she didn't realize we had been sitting next to her the entire time.

One event of this kind stands out because it was especially healing for me, and I sense for our daughter Kristen as well, who by this point had moved in with us to help care for her mom. The event occurred on Labor Day, three weeks before Margie's eventual death (and a week before she lost her ability to speak). My brother Bart invited me to come over for a barbecue with our extended family. Though I didn't want to leave Margie for any length of time, Kristen encouraged me to go and have fun. Knowing that she would take good care of her mother, and they would enjoy some one-on-one time, I decided to go to the outing with the rest of our family. Margie was supportive of me going, but I figured she would probably forget where I had been when I returned.

I was surprised by how much I missed Margie in those few hours of separation. During other seasons of marriage, we were both comfortable being apart. But in those final months, we had become so accustomed to each other's presence that it felt odd to be separated. Upon my return, I was astonished by how much she also seemed to miss me. She greeted me with exuberant joy, almost shouting with excitement, "Bob, you're home!" (It was as though I had been gone for months.) Just as quickly as she spoke those words of greeting,

she began to cry. "Where were you? I missed you." As she reached
her arms toward me, I came over to her in the wheelchair, and we
embraced each other tenderly. Then she began to sob uncontrollably,
saying, "Where were you? I missed you."

Kristen and I were shocked at the intensity of Margie's emotional response, and even more touched by her unrestrained display of
affection. Though she was often expressive of joy, it was uncharac-
teristic for Margie to be emotionally vulnerable in expressing her
sorrow and pain. In the moments afterward, she seemed somewhat
embarrassed over her emotional reaction. But for me, the encounter
was pure gift. After many comings and goings over the years, I don't
recall another greeting quite like this. I felt I was truly missed in my
going and genuinely delighted in upon my return. This interaction
brought me back to the memory of our passionate reunions when we
dated long-distance before marriage. Back then we felt so much joy
being together after months of separation. We were very conscious
of our need for companionship with each other.

Our Need for Companionship

Like Adam, we are all created with a basic innate need for companionship. We need to know that we belong and that our presence is
desired by another human being. When this need is not adequately met
within marriage, we become susceptible to searching for satisfaction
outside the marriage.[2] Conversely, when our need for companionship
is fulfilled, a continual sense of joy permeates the relationship. The
nature of companionship can involve a myriad of activities. But the
specific events are less important than the knowledge that someone
we care about desires our company and enjoys being in our presence.
This sense of joyful belonging is what makes daily companionship
so vital to a good marriage.

In comparison to the other key areas of communion, companionship often operates under the radar because it usually takes place in
the normal routines and rituals of daily life. Think about all the little
interactions we may or may not experience on a given day: a warm

smile, an affectionate touch, a soothing tone of voice, a loving glance, sharing a meal together, watching a favorite show, working side by side on a project, reading a book in each other's presence, having fun and laughing together. All these gestures and activities, and many others in the routines of life, communicate a simple but powerful message: "I enjoy being with you."

Many times, these ritual events may seem mundane, but they are nevertheless powerful in their impact. Catholic psychologist Dr. Gregory Popcak notes, "Rituals bind us together. They are more than mere repetitive actions. They have the ability to release spiritual power to create community and intimacy. Rituals of connection—regular activities that enable couples to work, play, talk, and pray together on both a daily and weekly basis—have incredible power to bind couples together."[3]

I didn't realize how powerful these daily activities of connection were until they were gone from my life. In the first weeks following Margie's death, the greatest feeling of missing her came from living these normal routines without her. When I went to bed each night and woke up each morning, I would look over and expect to see her lying next to me, just as she had for more than forty years. When confronted with the reality that she wasn't physically present anymore and wouldn't be, I felt as though a part of me had been ripped away. I had to come to terms with the fact that my constant companion, day and night, was no longer physically present in my life.

In her absence, I was surprised to discover the powerful reach of our companionship and how it had extended beyond physical space and distance. This realization struck me while traveling for the first time about a month after Margie's death. When I arrived at my destination, I instinctively picked up my cell phone to call her, as I ordinarily would have when she was alive. But this time when I started to call, I stopped abruptly, realizing she was not there on the other end to receive my phone call. Immediately noticing the void in the pit of my stomach, I released a whole new wave of grief. On my return home from the same trip, I felt her absence once again as I walked into the dark and lonely house, and I again grieved her absence.

Those experiences helped me realize the many ways I took our daily companionship for granted. I wasn't aware of how much those little moments of connection meant until they were not there anymore. I now have a better understanding of how the ongoing and repeated presence of our loved ones is what binds us together. More than anything else, companionship in marriage is simply a matter of being with each other, sharing time, space, and the ordinary activities of daily life. These normal daily activities create a sense of joyful belonging.

Joyful Belonging

When healthy companionship is present in marriage, it creates an environment where both spouses delight in each other, the way Adam delighted in Eve. According to the authors of *The Life Model*, being delighted in is a core human need for all of us: "Being human and wanting joy are inseparable. We are creatures of joy. At its essence joy is relational. Joy means someone is delighted to be with me!"[4]

This quality of joyful companionship is what Margie and I experienced at the beginning of our relationship, even before we started dating. It is one of the things that most attracted me to her. She exuded a joyful sense of welcome. I felt totally comfortable in her presence, which was unusual for me after having been wounded by my parents' divorce as well as by the betrayals from girlfriends in my earlier teen years. Before meeting Margie, I typically held back in relationships, especially with members of the opposite sex. It took me a while to open my heart and trust people. But with Margie, I felt at ease from the start. She emanated warmth. She was unassuming and real, which allowed me to relax and be myself. I knew immediately I could let down my guard in her presence. Evidently many others felt the same way around her. At her wake and funeral, we heard this repeatedly from family, friends, and even patients of Margie's. "Whenever I was in Margie's presence, I felt so personally loved and special to her. She would light up with joy and make me feel so wanted when she saw me."

Margie and I experienced many moments of joyful belonging, but we also both felt the lack of delight in each other's presence too many times. During the fall and winter seasons of our marriage, whether these lasted months or minutes, our being together stirred anxiety rather than peace. Not knowing where we stood with each other left us both in a state of emotional limbo. During those seasons, our gazes were shorter. We hugged and kissed less passionately and less often. We found it difficult to find things to do together that we both enjoyed. The net effect was that we didn't enjoy being around each other as much during those difficult seasons.

Have you ever felt like strangers in your own home even when your spouse is physically present? It can feel even lonelier than being totally by yourself. Many married couples are familiar with this experience due to a lack of fulfilling companionship. Marriage Encounter calls this state of coexistence "Married Singles." When we live two separate lives, we lose that special bond of love God intended for every married couple. That is why it is imperative you make companionship a priority.

Before considering how you can practically cultivate greater companionship in your marriage, let's pause a moment to reflect on your current experience of companionship.

Take a Moment

1. When you think of your daily companionship with each other, what shared activities do you find most fulfilling?

2. Have you ever felt lonely in your marriage? What contributed to it?

3. How important is daily companionship with your spouse in your list of priorities?

Reordering Priorities

Our priorities reveal what we consider valuable in life and how to order their importance in practical day-to-day living. Early in our marriage, Margie and I naturally placed a high priority on spending time together. We didn't even have to work at it. But then the demands of family life got in the way. You probably know the routine—school, work, children, chores, friendships, different interests, emotional distance, and so on. They all choked out our time and desire to be together. Before we knew it, we had lost our sense of connection and joyful belonging. This loss of connection became both the cause and effect of our depleted companionship. We had less time to do things together; but when we were together, we found it less enjoyable. We also found it more difficult to find things we really liked doing with each other during these seasons.

Our decline in companionship started when I was in graduate school and we both worked and took care of our young children. We didn't want our daughters to be in day care, so we staggered our work and school schedules so that one of us would always be home with them. Caring for our children was an important priority, but we neglected to prioritize our couple time together as an equally important value. During this season of our marriage, we began to spend the little available leisure time pursuing our own interests rather than doing things together. As a result, we grew further apart. I believe this was one of several factors that led to the difficult winter season in our late twenties and early thirties.

A few examples tell the story. On nights when I would study and the children were in bed, Margie would go out drinking with friends. I resented her "partying" with her friends, and these resentments built up over time. Similarly, she resented me studying all the time, and then spending all my free time in recreational activities with my friends.

Looking back, I can see that Margie made a lot of sacrifices to support me, including encouraging me to stay involved in sports because she knew I loved being active. I had played football throughout college. When it was over, I felt a big void in this area of physical activity. So, I found a flag football team, and my brother-in-law Nick (Kathy's husband) and I played together on the team. I found a lot of joy playing and hanging out with Nick and my other teammates. Our team finished third in the state tournament, which made it even more fun. But I didn't actively demonstrate my love for Margie as much as I "loved" my sports activities. She supported me playing but was not happy when I left her at home with a baby and toddler while I went out of town for three days to the state tournament. I chose my team and myself over her. My priorities were out of order. Rather than humbly acknowledge my selfishness, I proudly defended myself and ignored her concerns.

Years later, coming out of the most trying season of our marriage and refocusing my priorities in life, I knew I needed to make God my highest priority. But once again, I neglected the companion he gave me to cherish and nourish as my second most important priority. This time, though, I was under the false assumption that I was serving God. I became very active at church and left Margie and our young teenage daughters at home several nights a week. Again, I felt justified because (as I rationalized to myself and Margie) I was fulfilling my number one priority of seeking and serving God. Later, I realized that God wanted me to be at home more with my family. I had been putting my church and my own fulfillment above Margie and our children. I trust you see the point. Maintaining our priorities can be a lifelong challenge. It's not hard to see why Margie and I grew apart during those years.

Though my selfishness played a big part, I don't want to paint the picture that it was completely one-sided. Margie made similar choices in pursuit of her own happiness, choosing her friends and recreational activities over spending time with me and our family. We both failed to value our time together. We had our second most important priorities out of order.

Priorities are like beacons of light and guide rails that keep us on track going toward the destination we have in mind. We need to be clear about what we value most and keep our priorities in proper order. For Christian couples, priorities may look something like this:[5]

1. God: "Love the Lord your God with all your heart" (Mk 12:30).

2. Marriage—Spouse and Self: "Looking out not for his own interests, but [also] everyone for those of others" (Phil 2:4).

3. Children and grandchildren.

4. Extended family and friends.

5. Church, community, and ministry.

6. Work and career.

7. Recreation, hobbies, and other interests.

As you can see, every one of these priorities is important and has value. Agreeing on the order of priorities as a couple is not always the easiest thing to do. (It involves *cooperative teamwork*, which is the subject of the next chapter.) But even before you can come into agreement as a couple, you each must know for yourselves what you value most and then put those values into practice. Many of us have a gap between what we say we value and how we act on those priorities in our daily lives.

I remember attending a *Cursillo*[6] retreat weekend many years ago when one of the speakers said, "If you want to know your priorities, look through your checkbook. How you spend your money will tell you your priorities." There is a lot of truth in this statement, but it's not the full picture. The way we spend our money does say a lot about what is important to us. But equally important is how we spend our time and our energy, as well as our thoughts and the choices we make as a result of what we find important.

If we say that God is our number one priority but rarely spend our time praying and worshipping, we need to be honest with ourselves and acknowledge we are not living in practice what we profess to be important. Similarly, if we say we value spending time together as a couple, but in practice invest little money, time, thought, or energy in being together, we really need to reexamine our priorities. I would have told you that throughout our marriage, my relationship with Margie took second place in importance behind my relationship with

God. But there were many occasions throughout my life when I did not live these priorities in our daily activities. When things came to a crisis in my life, both God and Margie let me know I was not really devoted to them in the way that I promised I would be. To give Margie the proper value in my life, I was being called to cherish her as the precious gift from God that she was. I also needed to back that up in action by creating rituals and routines that would strengthen our bonds of companionship.

Rituals and Routines

According to Dr. Gregory Popcak, rituals and routines are the "skeleton" of a healthy and happy marriage. He underscores how essential these rituals and routines are for strengthening the bonds of companionship in marriage: "A couple may do many kinds of things together, but vitamin R, Rituals of Connection, helps guarantee that the skeleton that supports their relationship remains strong by identifying a baseline of daily and weekly work, play, talking, and praying activities that the couple commits to, come hell or high water. In doing so, the couple makes certain that their connection remains strong, regardless of how busy they become or how frustrated they might happen to be with each other."[7]

Rituals of connection are habitual ways of relating together around work and leisure. Some of these activities take place daily, while others take place on a weekly or monthly basis. Some can even be yearly rituals, such as putting up a Christmas tree or going on a vacation to your favorite locales. These rituals and routines are scheduled events that are given high priority. They ensure that a couple will spend time together in the ordinary events of daily life.

From the very beginning of our marriage, Margie and I struggled to find common ground regarding how to spend our leisure time together. I enjoyed reading, one-on-one conversations, playing chess, active sports, and vacationing in the mountains. Margie liked watching television, music, parties, shopping, and the beach. These differences remained with us throughout our entire marriage. Early on, we didn't know how to bridge these differences in order to find some common activities that we could enjoy doing together.

When we met in high school, Margie was a cheerleader, and I was an athlete. You name a sport; I loved playing it, and she loved cheering for it. We knew we had a common love for sports. But when it came to finding a way to connect with each other around sports, it was hard to find a shared activity that we both enjoyed. She enjoyed watching sports more than playing them. I loved playing sports and physical exertion more than watching them. When we were dating, I bought Margie a tennis racket so we could play together, thinking this was a sport in which we might be more equal in ability. But she was just beginning to play, and I had more experience, though it was not my best sport. When I hit balls to her, she would miss most of them and then go chase them. You can imagine it wasn't much fun for either of us. So after a couple of attempts, we gave up "playing" tennis as a couple.

Early in our dating and first years of marriage, we also tried shopping together. This was one of Margie's favorite recreational activities throughout her life. She loved to browse through department stores. When I shopped for clothing, which was very rare, I wanted to do it as quickly as possible. I preferred to go in, find what I wanted, buy it, and then get out as soon as I could. Our differences didn't make for great companionship while shopping. While she browsed, I stood around bored. When we went grocery shopping, she chose the brands she liked, no matter what they cost. I was more cost-conscious. Again, we discovered that shopping was not a good way for us to build bonds of connection.

Unfortunately, our lack of connection occurred over many different areas of our interests. Margie loved going to the beach and sunbathing. I tolerated it if there were other family members or friends there to play sports. She loved social gatherings and was usually the life of the party. I enjoyed solitude and one-on-one time. Early in our marriage, we tried going to parties with her friends at work (which I didn't enjoy) and later with my friends at church (which she didn't enjoy). I could go on with similar examples in housework. She liked cooking, and I wasn't much of a cook. I washed dishes instead. I cut the grass, and she trimmed. We complemented each other well, but we had trouble finding activities that we could share and enjoy. That is another one of the reasons we drifted apart. I imagine by now you are getting the picture and applying these examples to your own marriage.

After our crisis, we both saw how emotionally disconnected we had become. We desired to find more things to do together and to find ways to rebuild our bonds of connection. But we were at a loss as to where to start. We knew that we both liked doing things with our children and watching their activities at school and in sports. We also enjoyed watching some comedies and sporting events on television while sitting next to each other on the couch. We enjoyed sharing meals, watching movies together, and going out to eat. We always had a great time when we went on vacation. We both loved to ski and explore new places.

So these became some of our rituals of companionship. Some were daily, some weekly, some yearly. We had television shows we watched in the evening when we weren't at sporting or school events for our children (and then grandchildren). We went on dates almost every Friday night, often to dinner and occasionally to a movie. We went on vacation once or twice a year exploring different places, sometimes to the mountains, other times to the beach. Some of these were with our children, but some with just the two of us. We found our dates and vacations to be a good way to build bonds of connection. Through it all, we found it enjoyable just being around each other.

Now that Margie is gone, I will sometimes flip past one of her favorite shows on HGTV (Home and Garden Television) and remember the simple joy of those evenings sitting next to her, watching with her and rubbing her feet after her twelve-hour shifts as a labor and delivery nurse. Even if I don't miss watching those shows, I miss spending time with her, her cute little feet, and most especially the woman they belonged to.

I trust you hear how important it is for you as a couple to find those work and recreation activities that build your bonds of companionship. Working and playing together side by side (daily companionship) is just as essential for your marital happiness as praying and dialoguing together (spiritual unity and emotional intimacy). There is something deeply satisfying when couples can share a task together or play and laugh together. Even if there is not much verbal communication, there can be a great deal of contentment in just being with each other.

Let's take a moment to reflect on the rituals, routines, and priorities in your relationship. After the reflection questions, I encourage you to engage in the couple exercise, so you can plan rituals of connection that will strengthen your daily, weekly, and yearly companionship. This is an essential aspect of remaining devoted to each other.

Take a Moment

1. Make a list of your priorities as a couple. How well are you living these in practice?

2. What rituals and routines currently strengthen your bonds of connection?

3. In what ways do you struggle as a couple to find things you enjoy doing together? Are you devoted to improving this area of your marriage?

Activity for Couples: Working and Playing Together

1. (Husband) Begin by sharing a pleasant memory of working together. What did you enjoy in the activity? How did it foster companionship?

2. (Wife) Listen attentively to the reason why this was satisfying for your husband.

3. (Wife) Share a pleasant memory of companionship in a recreational activity. What made it enjoyable for you? How did it allow you to feel closer to your husband?

4. (Husband) Listen attentively to what made the recreational activity enjoyable for your wife.

5. Plan together an activity that you will do as a couple later this week to spend quality time with each other (it could be work, play, a date, or something else you both desire). Then, after planning, follow through and do it. Afterward discuss how it went.

6. Write out a plan to do something together every day, every week, and every year. Make a commitment. And then be devoted to following through on it. Possible ideas might include:

- Plan a date together.
- Agree on a work project together.
- Garden together.
- Cook dinner together.
- Volunteer together.
- Go shopping together.
- Play tennis, play golf, or swim together.
- Go to a movie together.
- Watch a favorite television show together.
- Read a book aloud together.
- Give each other a shoulder or foot rub.
- Go for a walk together.
- Work out at a gym together.
- Play a game together (cards, board game, etc.).
- Work on a scrapbook together.
- Watch a sporting event together.

6

SIDE BY SIDE: COOPERATIVE TEAMWORK

Be subordinate to one another out of reverence for Christ.

—Ephesians 5:21

Our daughter Carrie and son-in-law Duane are the parents of our eight awesome grandchildren—five boys and three girls—ranging in age from two to seventeen. They refer to themselves as "Team Daunt." (One Christmas, Margie bought them T-shirts with "Team Daunt" on the front and their birth order number on the back.) The team name originated from their love for soccer but has come to mean so much more in the way they live out their vocation as a family.

To manage a family of this size, Carrie and Duane have needed to excel in the area of cooperative teamwork. Like the rest of us, it is a work in progress, though they amaze me with how well they plan and work together and involve the children in the activities. The teamwork begins with Mom and Dad. When they are on the same page and living in the gift of their complementarity, everything else flows in unison. When they get out of sync, the rest of the family feels the effects. This is true for all families, because everything in the family flows from the unity and complementarity that exists between husband and wife.

Early in my marriage, I failed to appreciate that Margie and I were called to complement each other in our differences. Unconsciously, I wanted Margie to think like me, to be interested in all the things that brought me life, and to do things the way I thought they should be done. I naively thought, like many men of my generation, that this is what being "the head" of the family meant (see Eph 5:23). Like many modern women, Margie assured me that there was no way she was going to "submit" to me and do things my way (see Eph 5:22). So, at times I just gave in to her way of doing things to keep the peace. Neither way proved beneficial.

We both had a faulty understanding of the biblical injunction to be subject to each other out of reverence for Christ (see Eph 5:21). As a result, we remained susceptible to the twin curses of domination and control that began with Adam and Eve's original sin (see Gn 3:16–17). We struggled to come into unity because of these immature, sin-infected attitudes.

Recognizing our lack of teamwork, it humbled me to realize our selfishness was hurting our marriage and our children. In retrospect, I saw that each of us had been looking out for our own interests and inattentive to the other's needs and desires. In the process, we were neglecting the well-being of our family. Though if you would have asked me, I thought we were caring for our family the best way we knew how. We still had a lot of growing up to do. We both needed to mature in our capacity to love and cooperate.

Sobered by these realizations after my deeper spiritual conversion, I became more intent on seeking the Holy Spirit for guidance and strength in order to be more unified with Margie. He answered my prayers in many ways, but one of those ways completely amazed me. One day, while I was at a meeting with a friend at a church gathering, a woman who knew nothing about me spoke words that seemed to come directly from God. As soon as she began to speak, my heart felt as though it had been set on fire. I could sense the Holy Spirit speaking to my spirit as she proclaimed this message (which someone wrote out for me to keep):

> Son, I am putting key things together that strength
> might not just be strength upon strength but it might be

complement to complement. I do not need to put the same things together. I need to put diversified things together to bring the greater complement. And so, the Lord says that I've put you even in some situations where these things seem to be a struggle: "We don't think the same, we don't plan the same, our goals aren't the same." But the Spirit of God says this doesn't mean you are in the wrong place; it means you're in the right place. Son, rather than being the one who just feels the pressure to do it another way or one who feels like you have to push for your way, let there be a blending, let there be a strengthening.

Have you ever had an experience like this, when someone speaks about things that only God could know? It certainly gets your attention. Having felt so alone during those dark winter months of our relationship, it touched me to the core knowing that our heavenly Father intimately cared about our marriage and saw the silent struggles of my heart. As I received this message through the mouth of this modern-day prophetess, I knew beyond a shadow of a doubt that God had heard my silent prayers. Only God could have known me so intimately and spoken to our situation with such clarity. Though corrective in nature, his words comforted and encouraged me (see 1 Cor 14:3). Reaffirming that our marriage was not a mistake, he told me, "This doesn't mean you are in the wrong place; it means you are in the right place." For several years, I had believed the lie that our lack of unity was because we were incompatible and that our marriage had been a mistake.

In the light of this prophetic message, I could finally see that our lack of unity was due to our selfish attitudes and unwillingness to submit ourselves to God's way of doing things. When there was conflict, I had often oscillated between two extremes: either conceding to do things Margie's way or pushing to do things my way. As you can imagine and perhaps identify with, we both came away feeling resentful that our voice was not being heard and our interests were not being considered. Simply stated, we were failing to come into unity in this critical area of cooperative teamwork.

These resentments agitated each of our hearts and almost destroyed our marriage. Neither of us wanted to be subject to the other's control in any form or fashion. We hadn't yet learned how to blend our individual strengths to complement each other the way God intended. We had no real understanding of what it meant to "be subordinate to one another *out of reverence for Christ*" (Eph 5:21, emphasis added).

Reverence for Christ

During this accelerated season of spiritual growth and healing in our marriage, God continued to call me out of my self-focused ways of doing things while teaching me Christ's self-giving love as a pattern for my life. These changes impacted my life inside and outside of our home. As one example, I felt called, along with some cherished friends from my Christ Renews His Parish community, to go down to the inner city to minister to chemically dependent homeless men a few times a week. This required some significant sacrifices for each of us—impacting the income and the lifestyle of our families.

One friend, an attorney, moved from his million-dollar home, with his family of six, to a medium-sized apartment on the edge of the impoverished neighborhood where the halfway house was located. Inspired by the examples of St. Francis of Assisi and St. Teresa of Calcutta, he wanted to get out of debt and be more available to respond to the needs of the poor and oppressed. He worked part-time in his law practice and spent the rest of the time caring for the men at the halfway house. His whole family agreed with this major life choice.

Another friend had just built his dream house. After hearing Jesus speak clearly to both him and his wife, they sold their new house and moved into an apartment with their three young children. Soon after moving, he lost his job, and the profits from their recently sold house sustained them for six months, until he could find another job. They saw this as the Father's way of caring for their family. He spent his free time searching for a job and ministering at this halfway house with us.

A third friend, who had recently entered the empty-nest stage, also moved with his wife into a smaller home. Like my other two friends, he and his wife were in complete agreement on these moves. At the time, Margie and I, along with our two school-aged daughters were living in our small (1,100 square feet) but comfortable three-bedroom house. Our home served our needs well (or so I thought), but it became a bit crowded when two of my brothers moved in with us for about six months. Still, I felt satisfied we didn't need to downsize as my friends had done.

Unlike my friends and their wives, Margie and I were not in agreement about our housing situation. For Margie, our current house was a "starter house." For me, it was our first and only home. Our mortgage payment was $600 a month. With our modest income, we were able to make ends meet without accumulating any debt outside our mortgage. This was an important value for me, since in my family of origin we lived on food stamps after my dad left. By keeping our expenses low, I could give up two days of income to serve the men coming out of prison. Helping them get free of their addictions meant a lot to me, since both Margie and I had brothers who had been addicted to alcohol and drugs.

I was happy with our living situation and the freedom it afforded us. I merely wanted Margie to get in agreement with what *I thought* God wanted, just as my friends' wives had done. I admired their mutual submission, which had clearly come about as a result of their reverence for Christ (see Eph 5:21). Margie and I, on the other hand, were greatly lacking in spiritual unity and in this virtue of mutual submission. As a result, we were having trouble cooperating and working together as a team. We were locked in an ongoing *battle of wills*.

A Battle of Wills

Margie and I had very different perceptions and attitudes about our living situation, along with many other things. When I shared with her the choices my friends were making, she felt threatened that I might do something similar without her consent. She already expressed frustration about me taking income away from our family by giving up two days of work. She wanted us to move into a *bigger* house, not into a smaller dwelling as my friends had done. I tried to reassure her our house was the right size already and I had no intention of moving unless God made it clear that this was what he wanted.

She tried to tell me repeatedly that our house wasn't big enough for our needs, especially when caring for members of my family in addition to our children. Yet I didn't really listen to her reasons for wanting a bigger house. I quickly judged she was being greedy and too easily influenced by our American consumerist culture. Hypocritically, while judging her, it was me who was not *reverencing Christ*. During our conflicts, we each stubbornly held on to our willfulness, without listening to the other's concerns or desires.

Our opposing desires weren't the real problem; it was our unwillingness to submit these desires to God and to each other that kept us at odds with each other. We both held stubbornly to our positions without budging. Each time Margie brought up the subject of wanting a new house, I would immediately shut down the conversation with these words: "We can't afford a new house." She would respond accusatorily, "If you would work five days a week, we could afford another house." I would bluntly respond, "We don't need another house," and then abruptly walk away. End of conversation. Until the next go-round.

In these arguments, I deluded myself into believing I was being reasonable and faithfully handling our resources. I was totally blind to the fact that my stubborn refusal to discuss the issue with Margie was a form of male domination and control. In my attitudes and actions toward Margie, I was acting more like fallen Adam (see Gn 3:16) than like Jesus, the New Adam, who I said I wanted to emulate. Likewise, Margie was acting more like fallen Eve, grasping for what she wanted, and not like Mary, the New Eve, surrendering her will to God's will. I really believed I was in the right. Worse yet, I was certain God was on my side. As it turned out, I was wrong about that and a whole lot of other things.

This conflict between us came to a head when we invited my entire family to celebrate Christmas in our home. The occasion marked what we thought would be my brother Dave's last Christmas before he died. (He ended up making it one more Christmas before dying of AIDS contracted through a heroin needle.[1]) The gathering included my parents, my six siblings, and their spouses and children—about twenty-five people in total. You can imagine how we filled up all the spaces in the small living area of our home. Margie, who ordinarily loved to serve, felt the brunt of the cramped quarters trying to prepare meals in the tiny kitchen area with family all around. She hid her frustrations well, because I was oblivious to her anguish until after everyone was gone.

When I finally dropped off my father at the airport on New Year's Eve, I couldn't wait to get back home to view the video recording of our Christmas celebration. As Margie and I sat and watched, I felt a welling up of joy and gratitude for our time together as a family. I was amazed at how well it had gone. I had been concerned it would be awkward for all of us with my divorced parents in the same house for six days, but everyone responded graciously and with genuine love. We truly celebrated Christ's birth and the gift of our family, even with its brokenness and impending loss.

Unbeknownst to me, while I was basking in the moment of watching the video of our family gathering, Margie sat beside me fuming. All she could see on the video was the sea of family members swarming about in the tight quarters in our tiny living room and kitchen. Oblivious once again to her internal thoughts and nonverbal cues, I turned to her and said, "This was the best Christmas yet. Thank you for all you did—" Before I could finish my sentence, all her pent-up anger and frustration came boiling to the surface. "I'm glad it was good for you and the rest of the family. Do you have any idea what it was like for me to cook and serve everyone in this small house?" Rather than listen to her frustrations, I took offense to her comments. I couldn't believe her insensitivity (and she probably couldn't believe my lack of sensitivity to her). I thought to myself, *Here you go again, wanting a bigger house*. And then I responded out loud, "Why do you have to ruin this special occasion?" With that, I got up angrily from the couch and began making my way on a long walk around the block. It turned out to be one of the most important walks of my life, because I finally learned the wisdom surrounding *mutual submission and cooperative teamwork*.

Before sharing my discovery and its impact on our marriage, let's take a moment to reflect on how all this applies to you and your marriage.

Take a Moment

1. Do you recognize a "battle of wills" in any area of your marriage? Where do you need to improve your teamwork?

2. In what ways are you each grasping for control and dominating by imposing your will? In what ways are you conceding without full agreement? How do you feel when this happens?

3. What is your understanding of "mutual submission"? Do you believe it is essential for developing cooperative teamwork in marriage?

Mutual Submission

Mutual submission (out of reverence for Christ) comes about when we surrender our individual wills to God's holy will. This is the only way to effectively overcome the "battle of wills" that so easily impedes our unity in decision-making. In doing so, we let go of our demands and blend our strengths and unique insights while drawing on God's grace and wisdom. This act of subjecting our "wants" for the common good lies at the heart of the gospel message and is the key to developing cooperative teamwork. Can you imagine a sports team where everyone on the team has their own idea of how the plays should be run? Or an orchestra where everyone plays without concern for the conductor's direction? That would make for a lousy team and some rather irritating music, if you could even call it that. A similar thing happens in marriage when we insist on our own self-will. Self-centeredness fosters self-reliance and greatly hinders our ability to achieve our common goals and priorities.

This is where Margie and I were in many areas of our marriage before I took that life-changing walk around the block. I departed from our confrontation angry and hurt. I could tell Margie was also hurting. But I was too wrapped up in my own feelings to attend to hers. So, as I started to walk, I began to pray, asking God to lead us both. In praying, I realized we were stuck in a power struggle. Yet I couldn't see any way out of the dilemma. Even if one of us conceded and the other got their way, one of us would continue to feel resentful.

Turning again to prayer, I had an inspired thought (which I sensed was from the Holy Spirit). "Surrender this whole issue to the Father." Immediately I felt a supernatural peace replace my feelings of anger, confusion, and hopelessness. From this newfound peace, my prayer flowed freely from my heart and lips: "Father, I surrender our housing situation to you." I then felt remorse over how I had left Margie at the house. So I hastened my steps toward home. Upon my arrival at the house, my gaze met Margie's, and with newfound humility I said, "I'm sorry for being so insensitive to what you were going through. On my walk I realized that I am being stubborn and imposing my will on you. I decided to surrender the entire issue to God. I'm willing to discuss this again if you want to."

At first, Margie didn't say much. She was probably unsure whether to trust my sudden about-face. But at dinner later that night, she said, "I appreciate you being open to discussing the house. I'm going to surrender it to God too." Her response shocked me. But from that moment on, we both felt a new freedom to talk about our housing situation. I could finally hear it was not greed or envy motivating her to want a bigger house. She loved entertaining and caring for our extended family but explained to me how hard it was in our small house. I finally listened and heard her, without becoming defensive. In response, I told her about my friends' motivation in wanting to follow God's will. I explained why I didn't want to get into debt or be forced to work more and be away from family and ministry. She told me about her fears that I would give up everything to follow Jesus more radically like my friends did. I told her I wouldn't do anything without her blessing. We both listened and took to heart what the other thought and felt. We both experienced a major shift not only on this issue but in our teamwork in other areas of our life together.

I believe God received our mutual surrender as a gift of love for him, as well as for each other. He then showed us how intimately he is involved in these marital decisions. Having surrendered our will to his, he was free to move powerfully in our situation for our good and his glory. Our conflict, which had been going on for the past five years, resolved quickly. Within three weeks, we found a larger house that we both loved. It had a huge twenty-four-square-foot family room and a large kitchen and dining room area. It would be more than enough for our family's needs and perfect for Margie's entertaining. But there was one last issue we didn't know how to resolve. The house cost twice as much money as our previous house. We wouldn't be able to afford the mortgage and didn't have any money for closing costs. Yet, strangely, despite these obstacles, we both felt it was to be our new home. I was amazed at how peaceful we each felt, trusting that God had an answer.

He certainly did. In response to our trusting him, our heavenly Father stepped in, showing us that he was more than capable of working out all the details. Within the next twenty-four hours, he worked one small miracle after another. First, the owners of the house dropped the price by fifteen thousand dollars. They also said they would pay closing costs. We were amazed and grateful, but that still wasn't enough for us to afford the mortgage. Then, unexpectedly, the interest rates dropped 1 percent overnight. That lowered our mortgage significantly. With that, our monthly payments would be exactly what we originally thought we could afford. Recognizing God's hand in it all, how could we say no? But even with that, he wasn't finished showing us his extravagant love. The next day, we received $7,000 unexpectedly from a small investment (of $700) I had made a few years back. That extra money covered the closing costs for my sister to move into our old house, without us having to hire a realtor or find a buyer. All of this occurred within a day of us finding our new home.

God indeed had revealed his glory and his love for us. It was obvious to both of us that he had intervened in an amazing way. This strengthened each of us in our faith, and it let Margie know that both her heavenly Father and her husband cared deeply about her interests and desires. This time, we made sure to have our house blessed by a priest as soon as we moved in. For the entire time we lived there we felt great peace and a blessing on our marriage and family life. We stayed in that house until our daughters left home and completed college. Then, in full agreement, we downsized a bit.

As all these events unfolded, I realized that I had been completely mistaken in thinking I knew what God wanted for our family. I had been operating in proud presumption, not faith. After these events, I realized that our Father first wants us to hallow his name and then to trust him to provide our daily bread. This is his will—for us to be in unity with each other "out of reverence for Christ." He wanted me to love Margie and to bless her by meeting the desires of her heart. He also wanted to pour out his abundance on us, with way more than I thought we needed. Through the whole ordeal, I learned that you can't put God in a box. He does not operate according to our preconceived ideas of him. And ultimately I learned that his ways are the only way to happiness and harmony. We discovered that in subjecting ourselves to each other out of reverence for Christ, we both benefitted, and so did our daughters and our entire family. No one lost anything. We all won. Neither of us gave in or forced the other to do our will. We came into genuine unity through what I soon learned to refer to as an *enthusiastic agreement.*

Enthusiastic Agreement

A short while after this experience regarding the house, I ran across a book by marital therapist Willard Harley. *Give and Take: The Secret to Marital Compatibility*[2] describes a process of couple negotiation that seemed eerily like what Margie and I experienced when we discovered the art of mutual submission. He emphasized that enthusiastic agreement is the only way of maintaining genuine unity. He also spoke about many of the pitfalls that Margie and I had too easily fallen into, and then gave guidance for how to overcome them.

In this book, Harley contends that each of us is a *giver*—part of us wants to give to the other person for their benefit—and a *taker*—part of us wants what is in our own best interest. He emphasizes that it doesn't work in marriage for one person to always be the giver and the other the taker. Nor does it work to constantly compromise on decisions where you each win some and lose some. He said this inevitably leads to discontent and can even erode love and unity in marriage. His contention is that for couples to keep love alive and preserve unity, they must be committed to value both their own interests and those of their partner. We must not settle on a decision unless both of us are happy with the outcome.

When I saw the phrase *enthusiastic agreement*, I recognized immediately this was the gift Margie and I received in our mutual surrender. We were both completely happy with our decision about our housing situation and felt the added peace of God's blessing upon it. Though we still had many unresolved conflicts in our marriage after that, we both saw the value of looking out for each other's interests, as well as our own (see Phil 4:4). We tasted the good fruit of mutual surrender and wanted more.

After further reflection, I realized this is what it means to "be subordinate to one another out of reverence for Christ" (Eph 5:21). When we honor Jesus as the center of our marriage, we are able to transcend our self-centeredness. We take on his character when we look out for each other's well-being and not just our own. According to St. Paul, this is how we can live in unity and peace with each other:

> Complete my joy by being of the same mind, with the same love, united in heart, thinking one thing. Do nothing out of selfishness or out of vainglory; rather, humbly regard others as more important than yourselves, each looking out not only for his own interests, but [also] everyone for those of others.
>
> Have among yourselves the same attitude that is also yours in Christ Jesus. (Phil 2:2–5)

It is impossible to be of one mind and heart unless we each imitate and incarnate Christ's Spirit by giving of ourselves for the good of the other. This doesn't mean we ignore our own interests, because in doing that we fail to love ourselves and eventually become resentful. But by regarding our spouse and looking out for their interests as well as our own, we love them as we love ourselves. Without looking out for each other's interests, our love is not true devotion but just another form of manipulation and self-seeking.

As we close this chapter, you will have an opportunity to practice mutual submission and enthusiastic agreement with each other. This may be the most challenging and rewarding of any of the couple activities you have practiced so far. You may come face to face with your self-centeredness and desire to be in control. But keep in mind, if your goal is to *be devoted* to each other, it's worth the struggle. Mutual surrender is the key to cooperative teamwork and true devotion. Be patient and start small. Before turning to the activity, take a moment to reflect on how well you currently practice mutual submission and enthusiastic agreement in your relationship.

Take a Moment

1. Can you think of a time when you and your spouse practiced mutual submission? What happened? Did you come into enthusiastic agreement?

2. Do you believe it is always possible to reach enthusiastic agreement? What prevents you and your spouse from reaching agreement on essential issues?

3. Are you willing to practice mutual submission to arrive at enthusiastic agreement in some moderate area of conflict between you? If so, I encourage you to follow the steps laid out below, in order.

Activity for Couples:
Mutual Submission and Enthusiastic Agreement

A. Choose Topic: Choose a topic to discuss, one you both are ready to address. Let it be an issue that is not one of your most difficult. Make sure you are both in enthusiastic agreement about the topic you choose.

B. Prayer: Each of you individually begin with a prayer of surrender (say out loud):

> Heavenly Father, I surrender my will to you. Help me to submit myself to you and to my spouse out of reverence for Christ. Help me to look out for my [husband's/wife's] interests as well as my own. Reveal your will to us. Enable us to reach an enthusiastic agreement, with you and with each other. I ask this in Jesus' holy name. Amen.

C. Share Interests and Listen: You will know you have surrendered your will by how well you are able to listen to each other and care about your spouse's interests as well as your own.

1. (Wife) Begin by briefly expressing your desires and concerns regarding this issue. The key is expressing not only what you want, but why it is important to you—your underlying *interest*. (For example: not "I want a bigger house" but "I want a larger house because I want to be able to entertain and this house is too small to do that; and when we moved into this house, I never expected it to be our final house."

2. (Husband) Listen to, reflect on, and affirm your wife's interests ("I understand you want [wife's interests] because [wife's reasons]").

3. When wife acknowledges feeling understood and affirmed, switch roles. (If not, clarify again until you feel understood and at peace.)

4. (Husband) Briefly express your desires and concerns on this issue. Focus on why it is important to you—your underlying interest (e.g., "I don't want to move and get a bigger mortgage, because then we will get into more debt and have less freedom to do the things that are most important to us").

5. (Wife) Listen to, reflect on, and affirm husband's interests. ("I understand you want [husband's interests] because [husband's reasons].")

6. When husband acknowledges he feels understood and affirmed, go on to next step. (If not, clarify again until you feel understood and at peace.)

D. Seeking God's Will

1. Now that you have heard each other's interests, take time to pray and ask God what his interests are in the situation. (You may take some time to listen in prayer or reflect on scripture before continuing the discussion. Many of us have trouble trusting that we can hear from God. If you don't "hear" anything clearly, then

share what you think God might be saying to you. Another way of "hearing" God is to consider what it might mean to do God's will and love each other well in the situation.)

2. (Husband) Share what you believe God's interests are in the situation (e.g., "I am not sure if this is from God, but I sense he wants me to stretch out of my comfort zone and to care for what you want").

3. (Wife) Share what you believe God is saying about his interests (e.g., "I believe God is saying he wants us to be in unity with each other and to do what will be in the best interest of our marriage and our children").

4. See if you can take what both of you hear and combine them. Each of you takes a turn summarizing what you are hearing God speak through both of you. What do you believe is his will and desire?

E. Seeking Enthusiastic Agreement

1. Ask the Holy Spirit to guide you in your discussion.

2. (Husband and wife) Continue to dialogue about possible solutions, considering all three sets of interests, both of yours and God's.

3. If you have successfully walked through the previous steps, this process should flow freely and not become yet another battle of wills.

4. Stay the course until both of you are in enthusiastic agreement.

5. If you get stuck, go back to previous steps to see what is missing.

6. When you come into agreement, check to make sure you are both enthusiastic and at peace with it.

7. Thank God for his presence and his help.

8. Test the agreement over time. If it is truly enthusiastic, you will both continue to feel happy about it and to see the fruits of a good decision—love, joy, and peace.

7

BODY AND SOUL: SEXUAL FULFILLMENT

*Let my lover come to his garden
and eat its fruits of choicest yield.*

—Song of Songs 4:16

The Song of Songs is an erotic love song, championing the splendor, passion, and fulfillment inherent in sexual lovemaking. Commenting on the Song in his treatise on the theology of the body, Pope John Paul II remarks, "We find here [in the Song of Songs] . . . the themes that fill the literature of the whole world. The presence of these elements in this book that enters into the canon of Sacred Scripture shows that they and the related 'language of the body' contain a primordial and essential sign of holiness."[1]

If we properly understand the "language of the body," we can see that man and woman are "made for each other." God created male and female in such a way that sexual union is meant to be a source of intense pleasure, nourishing intimacy, and abundant fruitfulness. The key to sexual fulfillment is following *God's intention*. Deep and lasting satisfaction in sexual lovemaking is only possible to the extent that we engage in it according to God's design. "Sexuality . . . is realized in a truly human way only if it is an integral part of the love by which a man and woman commit themselves totally to one another until death"(*Familiaris Consortio* 11).

Considering all we have discussed so far, sexual lovemaking is meant to bring us into deeper communion with God and with each other by imaging Christ's self-giving covenant love, offered *freely*, *fully, faithfully,* and *fruitfully.* We will consider each of these characteristics of sexual love separately, beginning with *loving freely.*

Loving Freely

To be mutually fulfilling, sexual lovemaking requires free choice by both partners. It ceases to be genuine love when it is coerced, manipulated, or engaged in compulsively. Coercion in the bedroom (or anywhere else) is a violation of the dignity of both persons, and thus no longer an expression of authentic love. St. John Paul II insightfully observes, *"Man is a person precisely because he is master of himself and has dominion over himself.* Indeed, insofar as he is master over himself, he can 'give himself' to the other."[2] The virtue of self-mastery protects both husband and wife from acting compulsively and thus violating their partner's freedom, as well as their own.

Throughout my years as a marital therapist, I met with many couples who struggled with sexual compulsivity in one way or another. Many lacked self-mastery over their sexual desires and behaviors; this lack of freedom often hindered their sexual enjoyment as a couple. Men often came in unhappy with the frequency or active participation of their wives in lovemaking. They expressed the desire for their wives to be more interested and more passionate in their sexual expression. Many of these wives confirmed a loss of sexual desire due in part to their experience of feeling used. After exploring the reasons behind these complaints, typically one or more of the following issues came to the surface: (1) a history of pornography, sexual fantasy, and masturbation on the part of the husband and sometimes for the wife as well; (2) a history of sexual activity outside of marriage by one or both spouses (premarital sex or adultery); and (3) a history of sexual abuse or rape earlier in life, for one or both of them.

In each case, sexual compulsion was the underlying culprit. Sooner or later, lustful overtures by either member of the couple or by a third party took away the couple's freedom to have healthy sexual desires and engage in loving sexual activities within their marriage. This is a universal problem. Lust robs intimacy because it manifests as a grasping for pleasure while disregarding the freedom, dignity, and "inviolability" of the sexual partner. Christopher West notes, "To recognize the inviolability of a person is to recognize the unique inner mystery of that person and to commit oneself to honoring it. Authentic love, as John Paul II tells us, allows us a kind of 'entering' into the mystery of the person without ever violating the mystery of the person."[3]

When lust dominates the sexual relationship, it is inevitable that one or both parties will eventually experience sexual compulsivity and a loss of freedom in their sexual desires and behavior. The husband may lack freedom in mastering his sexual impulses by pressuring for sex or through premature orgasm. By contrast, the wife may lack the freedom to fully experience sexual pleasure or an inability to let go enough to experience orgasm. Though these two responses seem opposite, both are expressions of sexual compulsion. This is the normative pattern, but both men and women can be compulsive in either direction. Either one can have a compulsion toward sexual pleasure or a compulsion to avoid it.

Sexual compulsivity is much more common than you might expect. Few of us come into marriage completely pure and undefiled in the area of our sexuality. That is why healing of our sexuality is necessary for most couples before they get married, as well as once they are married. Before marriage, I naively thought I didn't need healing in my sexuality, but I discovered later in marriage that I was carrying baggage from the past that needed to be addressed.

These wounds came from my father's adultery, my mother's unmet emotional needs, my first two girlfriends' betrayals, and my own sins of impurity. My father's adultery and my girlfriends' betrayals created deep wounds of rejection and mistrust in my heart. My mother's needs led me to pull back in self-protection. As a result of all these together, I had a hard time trusting Margie and giving my heart to her. Furthermore, I felt insecure and jealous any time Margie would express affection toward another man. When I received some measure of healing, I experienced more freedom in my sexuality and could trust Margie more readily.

I also had self-inflicted wounds from viewing pornography in grade school. When I was eight years old, a friend showed me *Playboy* magazines he found in his brother's room. Even though I knew it was wrong, I engaged in looking at the images of naked women. I stopped looking at these pornographic images by eighth grade and didn't struggle with pornography after that, but it still had a hidden impact on the way I looked at and related to women. Before marriage, it fed my lust in relationships with girlfriends. After marriage, it influenced my way of relating to Margie in our sexual intimacy. Several years into our marriage, I finally faced these sins. As I did, I also acknowledged the ways Margie and I violated God's will by being sexually active before marriage and by practicing contraception and sterilization. I discovered, through the Holy Spirit's promptings, that these were areas where we both lacked freedom and needed healing.

I am grateful for that time of purification and forgiveness because it allowed us to enter a more trusting and open sexual relationship for our remaining years. Both of us were able to live in a greater measure of freedom while respecting the "inviolability" of the other. This, in turn, enabled us to give ourselves more fully to each other in lovemaking. Loving freely and naturally allows us to love more *fully*.

Loving Fully

Loving fully means participating in sexual intimacy with your whole being—body, soul, and spirit, without holding anything back. As such, it naturally involves all the areas of marital communion that we have been discussing up to this point. Sexual intimacy builds upon spiritual unity, emotional intimacy, daily companionship, and cooperative teamwork. Each of these areas profoundly influences your capacity for sexual fulfillment in your marriage.

Sexual fulfillment is first and foremost the fruit of *spiritual unity*. Since God is the source of all true love, he must be at the center of your sexual relationship for it to be self-giving. That is why prayer is essential if you are to give yourselves fully in sexual intimacy. Have you ever prayed together before entering into sexual lovemaking? If not, I encourage you to do so. I never thought of praying before sexual intimacy until hearing people at the Theology of the Body Institute share about the sexual fulfillment they experienced by incorporating prayer. When I returned home from the conference, I felt a desire to put the advice into practice and experienced some of the most beautiful and fulfilling sexual intimacy in our marriage. After inviting the Holy Spirit, I felt a renewed reverence for Margie and a greater ability to give myself to her without holding back.

After that initial experience, I continued the practice of praying before lovemaking for the remaining years of our marriage. Each time I prayed, I experienced God's blessing during our lovemaking. By invoking the Holy Spirit, we welcome God's love, joy, peace, gentleness, and self-control into our sexual love. In this way, sexual intimacy becomes a form of prayer and worship, as we offer our bodies "as a living sacrifice, holy and pleasing to God" (Rom 12:1).

Giving wholeheartedly and passionately in sexual love requires vulnerability and trust. These attributes come from preexisting levels of spiritual unity and *emotional intimacy*. Catholic sex therapists Christopher and Rachel McCluskey explain:

> We have already noted that lovemaking as God designed it is rooted in a healthy covenantal marriage. This does not mean a perfect marriage, but one in which both partners are completely committed to each other for life and *to being known, which means being real, transparent, and intimate with each other.* Their relationship is built on trust, requiring absolute honesty. They are not afraid of each other—of being harmed, belittled, cheated on, or deceived. They know that their marriage is grounded in the Lord and that they can lean into it when they need strength, and it will sustain them. Sexual union is the outgrowth and expression of these things. If these characteristics are not present, the couple is not ready for a healthy sexual relationship. They need to focus on healing and

growth, in their ability to love each other in non-sexual ways first.[4]

The McCluskeys' insights ring true to both my experience as a marital therapist and in my own marriage. When Margie and I were most emotionally and spiritually connected and secure, we were most able to be open and fulfilled in our sexual union. Without an emotional and spiritual connection, sex becomes merely a physical act, which ends up diminishing rather than enhancing the emotional bond between husband and wife. Women seem to be especially affected when sex is entered physically, without a preexisting emotional and spiritual connection.

As a marriage therapist, I observed this pattern repeatedly. Without emotional intimacy, most women eventually lose interest in their sexual relationship with their husbands. This is true for many men as well. But the opposite is also common in a loving marriage—sexual intimacy can provide the emotional safety that allows husbands and wives to become more vulnerable and more emotionally expressive with each other. The chemicals released during the sexual embrace have powerful bonding power. Have you found these things to be true in your relationship?

Sexual intimacy becomes even more deeply fulfilling when *daily companionship* and *cooperative teamwork* are flourishing in marriage. Being one in mind and heart, while sharing in recreational and work activities, is the best kind of sexual foreplay. In their book *Love and War*, John and Stasi Eldredge explain,

> The coming together of two bodies in the sensual fireworks of sex is meant to be a *consummating act*, the climactic event of two hearts and souls that have already been coming together outside the bedroom and can't wait to complete the intimacy as deeply as they possibly can. . . . For a woman to give herself over to her husband fully—which is sex as it ought to be—he has to have won her heart and won it again if only in small simple ways today. If she is going to be able

to abandon herself . . . her man is going to have paid attention to the *relationship*.[5]

This is just common sense. How can you give yourself completely in lovemaking when disconnection and disunity are prevalent outside the bedroom? How can you give of yourselves sexually when you are holding back in the other areas of your marriage? I can remember at times feeling disconnected in my marriage with Margie. At those times, I rarely had a desire for sexual intimacy. Neither did she have a desire when she didn't feel cherished and nourished. But when we were in communion with each other in these other areas of our relationship, our sexual intimacy became a deeper expression of our heartfelt devotion for each other.

The key point to remember in loving fully is that sexual fulfillment is an expression of all five areas of marital unity. The more you give of yourself wholeheartedly to your spouse in body, soul, and spirit outside the bedroom, the more you will both come away fulfilled in your sexual intimacy. Before going further, let's take a moment to reflect on your personal experiences of loving freely and fully.

Take a Moment

1. On a scale of 1 to 10, how fulfilled would you say you are in your sexual relationship?

2. Do you experience the interior freedom to give yourself fully to your spouse in lovemaking?

3. What wounds or compulsions from the past or present keep you from freely engaging in sexual intimacy with your whole heart?

Loving Faithfully

Every time you express your love in sexual embrace, it is meant to be a renewal of your wedding vows.[6] When you make love, you are physically reaffirming your promise to "love, honor, and cherish" each other and to be faithful to each other for the rest of your lives. Have you experienced your sexual intimacy in this way—as a renewal of your vows and as your pledge of faithfulness to each other?

Nothing hinders sexual fulfillment in marriage more than infidelity. Adultery is the most obvious form of unfaithfulness, and arguably the most damaging. Having accompanied many couples through the healing process from the wounds of adultery, I can assure you it is devastating to all parties involved. A few moments of illicit pleasure for one spouse reaps months and sometimes years of deep anguish and pain for both. Unfaithfulness shatters trust between spouses and wounds both of their hearts. Anyone who has experienced betrayal like this realizes that these wounds run deep, devastating the marriage while sending ripple effects of suffering throughout the family and social network of the couple. (I experienced these deep wounds as a young teenager with my father's infidelity to my mother. I can only imagine how deeply it impacted her.)

In addition to adultery, there are many other ways spouses can be unfaithful to each other, even by the choices made before marriage. Are you aware that any sexual relationship you engaged in outside of marriage, even if it occurred before your marriage, is a form of unfaithfulness? If either of you became "one flesh" (1 Cor 6:16) with someone other than your spouse, you were being unfaithful to your future spouse, without even knowing it. What should have been reserved and saved exclusively for your spouse in marriage was given to someone else prior to marriage. That is one of the many good reasons why God forbids fornication, i.e., sexual intercourse before marriage (see 1 Cor 6:9).

I have counseled many people over the years who intuitively felt this as a betrayal of their marriage covenant, even though it happened before meeting their future spouse. If this has been your experience, please know that God desires to forgive you and to bring healing in this area of your life and marriage. Whether you realized it or not, you created an *unholy attachment* with someone and spiritually became one with them by engaging in sexual intercourse with them outside of marriage (see 1 Cor 6:15–20). For healing to occur, this needs to be confessed as an offense against God, your spouse, yourself, and the person(s) you were sexually intimate with outside of marriage. Then renounce the unholy soul ties that were established between you and any person you had a previous sexual relationship with, including fantasy relationships. (See the "Renouncing Unholy Soul Ties" prayer in appendix 2.) I have observed the good fruit that has come in marriages when these wounds are healed and these illicit attachments are completely renounced and forgiven.

Healing is also needed for a myriad of other kinds of unfaithfulness. Pornography, masturbation, emotional affairs, and all lustful thoughts and actions within marriage are ways of being unfaithful to God and to your spouse. Jesus said, "Everyone who looks at a woman with lust has already committed adultery with her in his heart" (Mt 5:28). Pope John Paul II caused quite an uproar in the media a number of years ago when he warned that even married couples can commit "adultery in the heart." He says this occurs anytime they approach their partner with lust, rather than love: "Adultery 'in the heart' is not committed only because the man 'looks' in this way at a woman who is not his wife, but precisely because he looks in this way at a woman. Even if he were to look in this way at his wife, he would commit the same adultery 'in the heart.'"[7] This obviously applies to women as well as men. Few of us can say we are completely free from lust and have never been unfaithful to God's plan for love.

We can also be unfaithful to our spouse in nonsexual ways, which then hinders our sexual intimacy. Dr. John Gottman stretches our understanding of unfaithfulness to include any acts of disloyalty or betrayal within the marriage:

> Although we tend to think of infidelity in sexual terms, an extramarital affair is only one type of disloyalty. . . . Betrayal is, fundamentally, any act or life choice that doesn't prioritize the commitment and put the partner "before all others." Nonsexual betrayals can devastate a relationship as thoroughly as a sexual

affair. Some common forms of deceit include being
emotionally distant, siding with a parent against one's
mate, disrespecting the partner, and breaking significant promises. The truth is that most of us are guilty
of faithlessness from time to time. But when either
spouse consistently shortchanges the marriage, danger
follows. In fact, the Love Lab research indicates that
betrayal lies at the heart of every failed relationship.[8]

These are sobering words, aren't they? Before judging our spouse
for unfaithfulness, we need to look in the mirror. I held on to judgments toward my dad, until I forgave him for being unfaithful to my
mom and all of us. I realized I had no right to stand in judgment of him
without first taking the log out of my own eye (see Lk 6:42). I needed
to look inside myself to confront my varied forms of unfaithfulness to
Margie, and ultimately to God. Distancing myself from her was the
biggest form of unfaithfulness. But I also was unfaithful to our vows
whenever I put school, ministry, friends, children, and relationships
with family members or others over Margie (and God).

Similarly, her choosing partying, friendships, and family members
over me were ways she was unfaithful to me. Every unkind word or
action toward each other, and every time we withheld love from each
other, were failures to love each other faithfully. I think it is safe to
say that most of us have been unfaithful in one way or another in
marriage. Who of us can say we have been totally loyal, completely
honest, and have constantly chosen our spouse over everyone and
everything else (but God)?

If any of this tempts you to self-condemnation, please know that
is not my intention. If you are feeling shame or guilt, I encourage
you to pause and ask for God's mercy and healing. It does no good to
condemn yourself or your spouse for areas where either of you have
been unfaithful. You can ask God and your spouse for forgiveness,
go to confession, enter a process of healing, and begin the process
of restoring trust again (see chapters 9 and 10). On the other hand, if
you are currently tempted to any kind of infidelity, I urge you to do

everything in your power to seek God's help, so you can prevent the pain you would inevitably cause yourself and your spouse, as well as any children you may have.

If you have already experienced infidelity, don't give up hope and don't give up on your marriage. In my years as a marital therapist, I met with many couples for whom infidelity had almost destroyed their marriage, but through therapy, a strong faith commitment, perseverance, healing, and forgiveness, the great majority of these couples were able to reestablish trust and regain a deep love for each other. It wasn't without a lot of hard work that involved facing their own and their spouse's deep suffering. I know from my own experience with my father's unfaithfulness that healing often takes a while for all parties involved.

We can prevent a lot of heartache by following God's design for marriage by loving each other faithfully. One of the main ways we remain faithful to God and our spouse is by loving them *fruitfully*.

Loving Fruitfully

Being fruitful is simply respecting God's order and design for sexual intimacy. After creating Adam and Eve, God invited them (and all of us) to participate with him in the miraculous act of *procreation*: "Be fruitful and multiply" (see Gn 1:28, 9:1; Ps 127:3). Throughout the millennia, God has not changed his mind about this fundamental purpose of sexual intercourse. Children are the most precious fruit of sexual love. Kimberly Hahn notes, "Children are only and always a blessing . . . and a gift from God."[9]

In our modern culture, with the onset of birth control, invention of sterilization procedures, reproductive technologies, and the legalization of abortion, we have almost entirely denied the indissoluble link between the unitive and procreative aspects of sexuality. In centuries past, the unitive aspect (i.e., marital communion) was underemphasized. Now the procreative aspect is diminished as our culture has become more and more obsessed with sexual pleasure for its own sake. In his book *Holy Sex!*, Dr. Gregory Popcak contrasts holy sex (God's design) and eroticism (self-pleasuring).

> Eroticism is "all about me" and how much I can get out of you without having to give too much in return (e.g., commitment, fidelity, or real love); it is terrified of children. . . . Holy Sex challenges lovers to see that the incredible power of their love for each other cannot be kept between the two of them. Holy Sex celebrates a love that is so powerful that in nine months it has to be given a name. Holy Sex taps into the creative spark of Divine Love that longs to create more creatures to love and allows men and women to glimpse the joy God himself experiences when his love bursts into life.[10]

Many of us must overcome eroticism on our way to realizing sexual fulfillment. Before we were married, Margie and I, like many unmarried couples, wanted to indulge in the pleasure of sexual intimacy (eroticism) without having to face any of the natural consequences (pregnancy and caring for children). We had watched others we knew experience the painful consequences of becoming pregnant before marriage. So, with my consent, Margie took the pill to block fertility.

We convinced ourselves we were expressing love, but in truth, we were allowing eroticism to govern our sexual desires. We feared having children before marriage because we were not ready to care for them. It's amazing what a difference marriage makes in this regard. Soon after getting married, our fears disappeared and we both had a strong desire for children. Within the first three years of marriage we conceived and gave birth to the two most precious gifts of our love—our two daughters, Carrie and Kristen.

But then, after having our second daughter, Margie gave in to fear again and decided she wanted to have a tubal ligation. Though I desired more children, I conceded to her decision after she told me she was afraid she would be overwhelmed by caring for more than two children. She didn't want to shortchange them, she said. So once again, Margie's fear of children, and my passive consent, cut us off from living in God's blessing in our sexuality. Without realizing it, we were saying no to God's holy will and to his design for authentic lovemaking. Unwittingly, we invited death and control into our sexual relationship rather than trusting in God's ways and purposes, which bring life and love.

Though we were totally oblivious to any consequences of our decision at the time, I can now look back and see that our choice to sterilize fundamentally changed our sexual intimacy and our overall marriage. We thought that blocking fertility would increase sexual desire and provide greater opportunity, but it had the opposite effect. We became less inclined to engage in sexual intimacy and more anxious when we did. I believe this was one of the hidden factors catapulting us into the fall and winter seasons of our marriage.

I am sad to say it took me many years, until our daughters reached their late teenage years, before I realized that Margie and I had sinned against God and against our marriage by agreeing to block our fertility. After reading Christopher West's book *Good News about Sex and Marriage* and then later listening to Janet Smith's talk *Contraception: Why Not?*, the Holy Spirit convinced me of the goodness of God's plan. I realized that our use of contraception and sterilization were acts of unfaithfulness to God, which resulted in eliminating the fruitfulness of our love. Not only did it close us to the gift of more children but it also closed us to the Holy Spirit and the fruits of love, joy, peace, and self-control in our marriage (see Gal 5:22–23).

When I came to this awareness, I grieved over the impact of our self-centered choices. I am eternally grateful that I was able to receive God's mercy through the Sacrament of Reconciliation. Later, I apologized to Margie and to our daughters. I wanted to make amends, but I didn't know how else to make things right. Margie did not share my viewpoints on these matters and, even if she had, her tubal ligation was irreversible. I didn't see a way to actively repent for our previous decisions.

After praying about it, I felt a strong sense that I could follow God's will by teaching others the truth I had discovered, starting with our teenage daughters. I was amazed at how open they were to hear about God's design for sexuality and how it immediately made sense to them. Now, many years later, both Carrie and Kristen and their husbands are faithful witnesses to life, each in their own way. Carrie and Duane have a "quiver full" (Ps 127). They have brought us all great joy with eight beautiful children who are being raised in a home where love and faithfulness hold central place. My daughter Kristen and son-in-law Stephen are equally dedicated to fruitfulness, though they have not yet been able to conceive after nine years of marriage. They currently demonstrate their love of fruitfulness in their ministry work with teens (including teaching them about the theology of the body), and in the abundance of love they show for their nieces and nephews.

Through God's graciousness, my decision to teach others the truth about our sexuality has revealed other fruits beyond our immediate family. I am aware of several couples who became open to life after previously having a vasectomy. They, in turn, have become compelling witnesses to the Gospel of Life (*Evangelium Vitae*). One of those couples, after their reversal surgery, conceived a fourth child and asked me to be their son's godfather. I am overwhelmed by God's goodness and mercy.

Fruitful love is beautiful at any age or stage of life. I heard one of the most compelling witnesses of fruitful love from a woman in her seventies at the Theology of the Body Institute. We were discussing the vulnerability and trust that is required in opening our sexuality to God's design for love and life. During the discussion, this woman stood up to share her personal experiences. The following is a paraphrase of what I heard her say that day: "There have been two situations throughout my life where I was most vulnerable and most open to God. At these times, I felt I was living fully in my identity as a woman. The first is when I opened my body and soul to receive my husband's love and his seed of life in our sexual embrace. The second occurred, nine months later, when I opened myself, body and soul, once again to receive and nurture the fruit of our love—each baby." She noted one act of vulnerability began with pleasure (sexual intimacy) and the other with pain (labor and childbirth), but both together have given her the greatest fulfillment in her sexuality.

What about you? What has brought you the greatest fulfillment in your sexuality? Do you see how sexual lovemaking, when practiced according to God's design, is an expression of your devotion to him and to your spouse? Let's take a moment to reflect on how you are loving each other faithfully and fruitfully. After reflecting on these topics, I invite you (married and engaged couples) to participate in the couple exercise—Hand-Holding and Gazing. It's a powerfully intimate exercise that could enhance your capacity for mutual fulfillment.

Take a Moment

1. How does having the insight that sexual lovemaking is a renewal of vows change the way you approach each other sexually?

2. In what ways do you need to grow in faithfulness in your marriage? How has unfaithfulness (of any kind or degree) hindered your trust and openness with each other?

3. What is your reaction to the statement, "Contraception and abortion invite death and fearful control into the marriage relationship"? Do you believe this is true? Explain.

Activity for Couples: Hand-Holding and Gazing

This exercise of holding hands and gazing into each other's eyes is intended to enhance intimacy and trust between you. I encourage you to practice loving each other freely and fully in this activity. Most couples are initially a bit uncomfortable gazing into each other's eyes for any duration, so this may be a stretch for one or both of you. If you have nervous laughter at first, it's okay. As you persist through the uncomfortableness, trust that you will experience a new level of intimacy.

1. Ask each other if you are willing to engage in this activity now.

2. If no, have a conversation about why you don't want to do so.

3. If yes, begin by asking the Holy Spirit to be present with both of you.

4. Set a timer for five minutes.

5. Then hold each other's hands (both hands) and tenderly and sensually communicate your love for your spouse through touch.

6. As you hold hands, lovingly gaze into each other's eyes.

7. Do not speak or kiss until after the exercise is completed; let your hands and eyes express your love.

8. At the end, share your experience with each other.

PART II
HEALING AND RECONCILIATION

8

UNDERSTANDING THE ROOTS OF CONFLICTS

[Love] does not seek its own interests, . . . it
does not brood over injury.
—1 Corinthians 13:5

Your marriage will largely succeed or fail depending on how well you understand and reconcile the unavoidable conflicts that are inherent in your relationship. No matter how compatible or incompatible you believe you are, some level of conflict is inevitable. How you understand and address these issues will make the difference between whether you have a good marriage or a poor one, or one that falls somewhere in between. If handled well, your conflicts will bring you into deeper unity and intimacy with each other. If ignored long enough, unresolved conflicts can become internalized, and cause one or both of you to withdraw your love. Understanding your conflicts does not mean that all of them are resolvable. In fact, according Dr. John Gottman's research, *most conflicts in marriage are not resolvable*. It's how we relate to each other during conflicts that matters most.

> Couples spend year after year trying to change each other's mind, but it can't be done. This is because most of their disagreements are rooted in fundamental differences of lifestyle, personality, or values. By fighting over these differences, all they succeed in doing is wasting their time and harming their marriage. Instead, they need to understand the bottom-line difference

that is causing the conflict and learn how to live with
it by honoring and respecting each other. Only then
will they be able to build shared meaning and a sense
of purpose into their marriage.[1]

Gottman's conclusion came after watching thousands of hours of
video recordings of married couples addressing conflicts. Most conflicts, he contends, are not about the surface issues, but rather often
involve "deeper hidden issues that fuel these superficial conflicts and
make them far more intense and hurtful than they would otherwise
be."[2]

After nearly forty-two years of marriage, and more than four decades of accompanying married couples in their healing process, I find
Gottman's findings both troubling and affirming. They are troubling
because we all desire to have our conflicts resolved, and it can be
painful and disquieting when they remain unresolved. But his conclu-
sions are ultimately affirming because they speak to the reality I have
experienced in my marriage as well as what I observed ministering to
hundreds of couples over the years.

Spouses have numerous differences in personality, values, life-
styles, and hidden expectations for their marriage. Many of these
differences will remain until they die. These fundamental differences
need to be understood and respected. It does no good to try to change
the fundamental nature of your spouse in order to make them think
and act more like you. That *never* works. Trust me, I tried many times
to convince Margie to think the way I think, and it always failed. Instead, as we discussed in the chapter on cooperative teamwork, these
differences need to be addressed with love, in a posture of mutual
submission, and with reverence for each other and for Christ (see
Eph 5:21). This process of mutual respect begins by recognizing your
fundamental differences in personality.

Personality Differences

In their popular book *The Temperament God Gave You*, Art and Laraine Bennett propose that temperaments are inborn. One person by nature may be more laid back; the other more intense. One is jovial and outgoing; the other more reflective. One speaks freely; the other rarely shares all they are thinking. You can see how these differences might play out in marriage—sometimes in very complementary ways, but at other times as a source of ongoing conflict and frustration.

At the beginning of a relationship, these differences are often complementary. Consider, for example, the partner who is more expressive and likes to share her thoughts and feelings, while the other is a good listener who enjoys processing things internally. This can be a near-perfect match—an example of how "opposites attract." This natural complementarity may play out in a positive way throughout marriage, but it can also become a source of pain and conflict if the couple doesn't learn to balance and compensate for their natural dispositions. Over time, the good listener may build up resentment about feeling unheard and misunderstood. Simultaneously, the more engaging communicator may resent not having as much dynamic interaction and feedback as they would like to maintain vibrant conversations in their relationship.

Like many couples, Margie and I had different but mostly compatible temperaments. Despite our compatibility, there were certain ways that our individual temperaments made it more challenging to face and deal with conflicts. With my easygoing temperament, I wanted everything to be harmonious, calm, and peaceful. Margie, with a fun-loving and outgoing temperament, liked things to be congenial and happy all the time.

Neither one of us enjoyed being in a state of unresolved conflict, which meant we didn't fight often. But when it came to addressing conflicts, Margie preferred (to use her terms) to "bury her head in the sand." That, by itself, created ongoing distress for me. I preferred to address our conflicts calmly and resolve them as quickly as possible in order to restore peace and harmony between us. Sometimes, when the conflicts were not addressed adequately, I would internalize them, which would disturb my peace of mind and eventually hers. This sometimes led to more intense conflicts, which neither of us enjoyed.

Temperaments make up a core part of each person's personality, but as the Bennetts clarify, temperaments are not synonymous with personality. Personality is a much broader construct that includes "the whole of the person's thoughts, behaviors, and emotions," which go into making up a person's overall *character*. Our temperaments are the fundamental building blocks of our personalities, but our choices, training, and culture also have a tremendous impact on our overall makeup.[3]

Personality involves our unique inborn temperament (nature) and our acquired character qualities (nurture). Both play an important part in marital dynamics. It is extremely beneficial to have a basic understanding of your own and your partner's temperament and character qualities before entering marriage. For this reason, many pastors and counselors encourage couples to take premarital and marital inventories to assess overall personality differences as well as other areas of compatibility. These inventories can assist couples in understanding and addressing the potential areas of conflict that will sooner or later surface in their relationship.

Two of the most well known of these inventories are Foccus and Prepare (for engaged couples) and Refoccus and Enrich (for married couples).[4] There are also other popular personality tests, such as the Myers–Briggs and the DISC assessment, which highlight several key facets of personality.[5] If you haven't worked through any of these inventories yet, I encourage you to do so. Then sit down with a pastor or counselor to go over your results. Understanding your basic personality differences should help you navigate your conflicts with greater reverence and mutual respect. Margie and I did not have these available before we were married. We had to gradually discover the differences in our respective temperaments and personalities throughout our marriage. Part of this discovery process was learning how our *gender differences* played an important role in our understanding of the world.

Gender Differences

There are many people and organizations today that downplay the importance of gender or want to deny there are any differences between men and women. But the popularity of bestselling books such as *Men Are from Mars, Women Are from Venus* and *Men and Women Are from Eden*[6] show that many married couples are quite interested in understanding the inherent differences between the sexes. Research has validated that there are fundamental differences in the way men and women relate in marriage.[7] And scripture highlights these differences in the creation story: "God created mankind in his image; in the image of God he created them; male and female he created them" (Gn 1:27).

I was amazed while studying the theology of the body to discover the rich meaning of the Hebrew names for male and female.[8] The word *male* in Hebrew is *zakar*. It literally means "to remember," and it speaks to the man's call to be faithful to God's covenant. Throughout salvation history, God consistently calls the man to be the *initiator of the covenant*. The Hebrew word for *female* is *neqebeh*, which is also rich with meaning. It means "open," and it speaks to the woman's *receptive and nurturing* nature and her role as *the initiator of communion*. As St. John Paul II observes, there is no greater human communion than that which a mother experiences with her child.[9] Can you see how the male remembering the covenant protects the vulnerable communion between mother and child, as well as that which exists between husband, wife, and children?

One example of our gender differences became apparent when our daughters were born. Having carried these babies in her womb and giving birth to them, Margie's love was more intimate than mine could ever be. She was fully engaged and had little concern for the future in that heightened moment of joy. I delighted in being present at my daughters' births and fell in love with each of them immediately, but no matter how hard I tried, I couldn't experience the level of communion Margie felt with them. I marveled at my wife's strength through labor and in giving birth, and at her bond with them immediately after birth. I too felt a bond, but it was different than the one they experienced as mother and child. Margie was on the inside of the experience, and I participated from the outside. On the other hand, I experienced my identity as a father immediately. Though I was still in school, I felt responsible as the primary provider and protector and had a long-term vision for their lives. Even though Margie shared equally in those roles, she did not carry the weight of them like I did as a man. We both loved our girls, but in different ways.

As men and women, we have much in common in our humanity. But we also have many attributes that are dissimilar due to our unique sexual design. The following are just a few of the many differences between men and women: DNA, reproductive anatomy, hormones, brain structures, sensitivities, intuition, and relational capacities. Did you know that men's and women's brains are structured differently? Interestingly, men have a thicker corpus callosum, which is the nerve bundle dividing right and left hemispheres of the brain. This is due to the male hormone testosterone, which is released early in fetal development.

One effect of this difference in brain composition is that men have a greater ability to compartmentalize. We typically process the interchange between thoughts and feelings much less quickly than women do. We also become overwhelmed in heightened conflict much more readily than women do.[10] That may be why, as some humorists contend, a husband can never win an argument with his wife. She processes information much too quickly for him to keep up. We may laugh at the comedian's insight, but it is no laughing matter in the middle of an intense argument. These differences between the sexes are meant to complement each other, but they can be a source of tremendous pain and hardship when not mutually understood and respected.

By contrast, men tend, on average, to be physically stronger than their wives. A man is naturally called to be the protector. But this strength can become a weakness when a man, feeling overpowered in the middle of a heated conflict, uses physical intimidation to over-power and silence his wife. Clearly this is an abuse of power and reveals a lack of internal strength in honoring the dignity of his wife.

If we don't recognize and respect these individual strengths and weaknesses, either side is prone to misuse their strength in the face of the other's weaknesses. Conversely, when the differences are respected, they become a source of complementarity and mutual support.

Gender differences can also influence the way we relate with one another, even in low-stress situations. In marital needs inventories, most women report that emotional intimacy and security are their primary needs in marriage. By contrast, many men tend toward non-verbal expressions in their pursuit of connection. They often prefer physical activity over intimate emotional sharing. Men are typically more inclined to seek relational connectedness in physical activities such as work and recreational companionship, and in sexual fulfill-ment.[11] These differences between physical and emotional expression are present even in early childhood. Comparative studies of boys and girls in unstructured situations typically reveal boys are more likely to bond through sharing in physical activities, while girls are more inclined to form relational bonds through verbal communication in small, intimate groups.[12]

Despite these overall differences in gender, Dr. Gregory Popcak cautions that we cannot fall into stereotypes. He notes that in about 20 percent of married couples, these patterns of relating seem to be reversed.[13] In these cases, husbands are more emotionally expressive, whereas their wives are more nonverbal in their pursuit of emotional connectedness. Every couple is unique. One of the many reasons for this uniqueness is that each of us has our own way of giving and receiving love. These expressions are referred to as *love languages*.

Love Languages

Gary Chapman's bestselling book *The 5 Love Languages* has been read by more than eleven million people throughout the world. It is consistently one of the bestselling marriage books on the market, indicating that it has resonated with many. In it, he identifies and describes five different ways of giving and receiving love that

Part II: Healing and Reconciliation

affect the way we interact with our family and friends. These love languages are:

1. *Words of Affirmation*—Using kind words and nurturing tone of voice to encourage the other person and affirm their goodness and accomplishments.

2. *Giving Gifts*—Concrete expressions of love in the form of money or material things with the goal of meeting a personal need or desire.

3. *Acts of Service*—Showing love by meeting physical needs or doing practical things to meet immediate needs, such as cooking a meal, washing dishes, vacuuming floors, or house repairs.

4. *Quality Time*—Being present and offering undivided attention as an expression of love, such as taking a walk together or sitting and listening attentively.

5. *Physical Touch*—Expressing love through physical touch, holding hands, hugging, kissing, or sexual lovemaking.[14]

Each one of us has the capacity to express love in all five of these ways. However, Chapman proposes that each of us has a primary love language. I have found that most people also have secondary and tertiary ways they prefer to give and receive love. These love languages are expressions of our unique spiritual gifting (see Rom 12:4–8). When you fail to recognize these differences in the way you are each gifted, you may come away from interactions feeling unloved and underappreciated.

Like many couples, Margie and I had different primary love languages. Though complementary, these differences were also a source of conflict between us. We often missed each other in our primary love language, but we found places to meet each other's love needs through our secondary love languages. Margie had an incredible gift of *service*. Whether with our family or at work as a nurse, she found great joy in serving others selflessly, and she did it with great love. She cared for people very actively, whether it was cooking a meal, starting an IV or assisting in a delivery as a nurse, or offering a helping hand to anyone in need.

Unfortunately, service is probably the least prominent of my love languages. While I admired her for this and benefitted from her loving me and others in this way, service didn't communicate affection to me. Neither did it come naturally for me to love her well in this area that she valued so highly. I had to learn over time how to consciously serve her in ways that communicated love to her. By cleaning the kitchen before she got home from work, I could tell her in a concrete way that I cared about her. She told me she became more attracted to me even when I did some small service, such as changing a light bulb in the kitchen. (That shows you how poor I was in this area and how little it took to say "I love you" in her love language.)

My primary love language is *quality time*. I'm a good listener and love one-on-one quality time with people. It usually takes me a while to open my heart to share intimately, but when someone takes the time to listen and be attuned to my needs, I enjoy receiving attention in this way. I also enjoy listening as they share. At those times, I feel deeply loved and known. Unfortunately, this was not high on Margie's list of love languages. So, I sometimes felt unloved when she didn't come and sit down and engage in a deep conversation or participate in a favorite activity of mine. At times, this created a sense of loneliness for me in our relationship. I wanted to have deep sharing together, but it was not a natural desire for Margie.

Thankfully, we were a good match in our secondary love languages, *physical touch*. From the very beginning of our relationship, we both enjoyed holding hands, cuddling on the couch, kissing, and hugging. Though we frequently missed meeting each other's needs in our primary love languages, we made up for it through this secondary love language of touch. This is one of the things I now miss most since Margie is gone—just sitting next to her and holding hands.

Discovering each other's love language, along with personality and gender differences, saves a lot of unnecessary conflict and misunderstanding. So, before going further, take a moment to see how you and your spouse differ in these areas. Then identify some of the

critical issues of conflict in your marriage, which we will address in
the second part of this chapter.

Take a Moment

1. Describe your differences in personality. How do your temperaments and gender differences influence the way you address
   conflicts in your relationship?

2. What is your primary love language? What is your spouse's love
   language? In what ways are these complementary? How do these
   differences in love languages create conflicts between you?

3. What are the critical issues in your marriage that threaten your
   unity? What conflicts are repetitive in your marriage?

Critical Issues

By the end of Margie's life, Margie and I still had many unresolved
conflicts between us, though we grew tremendously over the years
in our ability to honor and respect each other despite these many
differences. Some of our conflicts originated in personality differences, some in gender differences, and others from different values
and lifestyle choices. Underlying all these were our "deeper hidden
issues," which Gottman identifies as the most critical in marriage.
These deeper hidden issues included our respective areas of selfishness, sins, and wounds. These underlying issues fueled the surface
conflicts and made them far more intense and hurtful.

Most couples have difficulty accepting, honoring, and negotiating
differences when it comes to these "deeper hidden issues." Our fallen
nature has a basic core of self-centeredness that hinders our capacity to reconcile our differences and become more unified. We also
bring into marriage a whole lifetime of accumulated vices and selfish
behaviors that must be addressed and confronted in the day-to-day

conflicts that inevitably arise. It is vitally important to acknowledge these areas. As these are confronted, we come to realize that each of us has significant wounds and areas of sin that must be healed and forgiven before we can make peace with these unresolvable issues.

You and your spouse have thousands of differences between you, but only a small number of these are critical to your overall well-being as a couple and family. Identifying these critical issues will help you see what prevents you from enjoying greater connectedness and unity. Discovering the underlying roots of your repetitive conflicts will also reveal where your unhealed wounds and sins continue to undermine your marriage. Many authors identify lists of critical issues in marriage that can make or break a relationship. The "big three" that are listed by many commentators are *money*, *sex*, and *parenting*. These three issues are critical because they affect your livelihood, your relational fulfillment, and your family harmony. And all three have a significant impact on your marital unity.

You may or may not have strong feelings about each of these issues. But even if your values about these issues are relatively compatible, you will still have some fundamental differences in the way you approach these three areas. In addition to your differences in personality, gender, and love languages, you were each influenced by the way your family of origin handled these matters. Without fully realizing it, you internalized values of how to respond to these issues in the atmosphere of your home, school, church, and subculture while growing up. Some degree of conflict is almost inevitable because of the dissimilarities in your upbringing, personality, and perspectives. Moreover, these conflicts can become heated and problematic when contaminated by your individual areas of self-centeredness, sins, and emotional wounds.

Margie and I had conflicts involving all three of these critical issues (sex, parenting, and money management). Though we were fundamentally compatible in our sexual relationship because of our shared love language of touch, I carried some inner conflicts about sexuality into our marriage. I brought wounds of insecurity and mistrust into our relationship because of my father's infidelity and my first two girlfriends' betrayals. For the first ten years of our marriage, I had repetitive nightmares about Margie being unfaithful. With Margie's reassurance, I eventually realized that my conflict wasn't with her but within myself coming from past trauma.

Following a season of intense exploration, I discovered these unhealed traumas were accompanied by unforgiveness. These were the deeper issues underlying this area of conflict. I was projecting my fears of being betrayed onto Margie and selfishly trying to control her relationships with men as a way of protecting myself from being hurt again. It wasn't until God healed these deep wounds of betrayal and abandonment from my childhood that I could let go of my insecurity and trust in her faithfulness.

Regarding parenting, Margie and I had relatively few conflicts in the early years of our children's life. For the most part, we parented well together. But our conflicts increased significantly when our daughters became teenagers and began to rebel at times. When our children acted disrespectfully toward their mother, I failed to correct them. Worse yet, I encouraged them to express themselves, which infuriated Margie even more. Once again, I had to look inside my own heart before I could address this problem effectively with Margie. After prayer and self-examination, I realized this was an area of covert sin in my life originating from my own teenage years.

After my dad left, my brothers and sisters and I acted disrespectfully toward my mom. Without seeing the connection at first, I was letting our daughters disrespect their mom in a similar way. I wrongfully sided with them in their anger rather than stand in unity with my wife. Once I came to realize this, I had to apologize to Margie (and to God) and uphold her honor and authority by disciplining our children when they disrespected their mom. Before I saw my part in this dynamic, we had many arguments over parenting our teenage daughters. Once I made the shift in my thoughts and behavior, the disrespect in our home decreased significantly, as did the conflicts between Margie and me.

Finally, in the area of money management, we had ongoing conflicts throughout our marriage. Margie enjoyed shopping. But she didn't like to keep track of her spending and didn't mind using a credit card. I hated debt, handled money conservatively, and liked to give money to those in need rather than buying more for us. Margie resented my giving money to others when we had unmet needs as a family. Periodically, these issues would erupt in heated arguments. Paying our bills at the end of the month seemed to be a trigger for both of us.

After many unsuccessful attempts to resolve this issue, we finally grew in understanding of each other's perspectives, personalities, and wounds. Margie was naturally more inclined to spend than I was. But that wasn't the biggest factor in our conflicts. She shared with me her experience of watching her parents fight over the bills as a child. Her mom would spend money freely, often buying clothes for herself and her children on a credit card. Her dad would tersely question her mom about using the credit card, and Margie would see them fighting over money. Resenting her father for this, she unwittingly projected her resentments of her father onto me when I asked about receipts and credit card bills.

On my side of this issue, I realized that my mom, left without income, piled up debts after my dad left. I came to realize this influenced my fearful attitude toward debt and unrestrained spending. It also increased my compassion for those families without enough, which fostered my desire to give to those in need. These realizations helped take much of the heat and judgments out of our conflicts, even though the conflicts themselves never went away until the last few months of our marriage, when the only spending was on doctor's visits.

These "big three" critical issues of sex, parenting, and money may or may not be hot topics in your marriage. But I can assure you, you have some critical issues in your marriage that need to go through a similar examination. These critical issues may include friends, relatives, time management, work involvement, affection outside the bedroom, tidiness, honesty, addictions, unfaithfulness, and so on.[15] These are typical issues in marriage, but they may remain unresolved because of the underlying root attitudes that fuel the conflict and make it a problem area in your relationship. These underlying root attitudes, as I have been demonstrating, are often hidden from our sight. They involve our unhealed wounds, our unconfessed sins, and our habitual patterns of self-centeredness. Healing and forgiving these underlying root attitudes are the keys to unlocking your marital conflicts and building unity in your relationship.

Underlying Relational Issues

During my first year in graduate school, I learned a nugget of wisdom that remained invaluable throughout my marriage and served me well in my career as a family therapist. I don't remember the source of the quote, but the phrase is engraved in my mind: "If an argument lasts beyond fifteen minutes, you can be assured that the *content* is no longer the issue—the *relationship* has become the issue." The *content*—what Gottman refers to as the surface issues—involves the topical areas of difference you need to address in order to come to some level of agreement. But behind these topical issues, no matter what they are, remains a whole history of relationships, past and present, including your family of origin, previous friendships and dating relationships, and the entire history of your relationship with your spouse. These underlying relational issues are what Gottman meant when he spoke about the *deeper hidden issues that cause the most pain*. This is really where the problems emerge in marriage.

Have you noticed this reality in your conflicts? You may start off discussing an issue that needs to be addressed, but before long you find yourselves focusing on each other's character and a whole history of past hurtful interactions around this topic. You can't resolve the content of the issue because the relationship dynamics remain as obstacles in the way. I believe all of us have experienced these underlying issues repeatedly in our relationships. The real challenge is how we reverence each other when our individual needs and values are threatened. Most of us want to do better, but we have a whole history of unresolved issues holding us back.

We each have unhealed emotional wounds we brought into marriage. We also have a whole history of self-centered attitudes and behaviors that undercut our love for each other. In short, we're a beautiful mess. It's a wonder any of us makes it through marriage, considering all we must contend with along the way. But whether we like it or not, this is the reality of living in a broken world. You can blame your spouse, but it will only make things worse. You can blame Adam and Eve, who started it all by their rebellion, but all you need to do is look in the mirror to see we are more like them than we want to admit. Any time you don't trust God and do things your own way, you and your spouse become a carbon copy of that first couple who decided that they knew better than God. Like them, you may blame God or Satan, but deep down we all know we play the most important part in our problems.

I believe one of the reasons we don't take full responsibility for our part in the conflicts is that we feel helpless to do anything differently and are ashamed of our own behavior. Can you identify with St. Paul in this regard? "What I do, I do not understand. For I do not do what I want, but I do what I hate. . . . So now it is no longer I who do it, but sin that dwells in me" (Rom 7:15, 17).

I love how St. Paul acknowledges his failure to love and follow God's will, while maintaining his identity apart from his sin. He doesn't let shame define him: "It is no longer I who do it, but sin that dwells in me." We all need to face our sins and failures, but we are far more than our sins and failures. St. John Paul II proclaimed this message to the whole world during World Youth Day in Toronto in 2002: "*We are not the sum of our weaknesses and failures*; we are the sum of the father's love for us and our real capacity to become the image of his Son."[16]

It is humbling to face our weaknesses and our inability to love each other well. I desired to love Margie so much more than I did. My selfishness, sin, and wounds got in the way of being the husband I always wanted to be. Likewise, I desired to be loved by her far more than she was capable. We both fell woefully short of being perfect spouses. If the story ended there, we would have given up in futility and done what satiated our needs. That is what much of the world does, because they don't know the love and mercy of God. As followers of Christ, we have the assurance of God's mercy and grace. It is real and powerful and given to us freely through the sacraments. Through his grace we can remain devoted, even in the face of our weaknesses and failures in love.

In the next chapter, we will discuss how to apply God's mercy and grace in healing our hearts and marriages. As you prepare for those remedies, I encourage you to reflect on the critical issues in your marriage and the deeper relational issues that underlie these conflicts. The reflection questions and couple activity will lead you through the process of examining your conflicts.

Take a Moment

1. Identify a recurring conflict in your relationship.

2. What is the *content* issue? Write out your differing viewpoints on this area of conflict.

3. What are the underlying *relational issues* that prevent you from resolving this issue? What would it take for this relational issue to be healed and reconciled?

Activity for Couples:
Marital Conflict and Core Wounds

As you saw in the examples throughout the chapter, there are often core wounds and hidden sins that lie behind each repetitive marital conflict. But because they are hidden, we need help discovering them. So, as you engage in this activity, I encourage you each to ask the Holy Spirit to help you see these hidden issues within yourself and your partner. As you explore these hidden wounds and sins, do so with understanding and compassion.

Personal Reflection

1. Begin by reflecting personally on how you perceive your marital conflict. See it clearly in your imagination. If you were to draw a picture of you interacting during conflict, how would you depict each of you in the argument? In your mind's eye, pay attention to what each of you is expressing nonverbally through your body posture and facial expressions.

2. Once you can picture both of you in the scene, name the feelings that you observe in each of your faces and body postures. Write down what you believe each of you is feeling.

3. Now ask the Holy Spirit to show you when you had similar feelings as a child or teenager. Imagine a movie or illustration depicting you as a child or teenager in an interaction where you were hurt emotionally by your parents, relatives, teachers, coaches, siblings, friends, or someone of the opposite sex. What do you see? How do you feel? (You may want to draw or imagine this so you can visualize it.)

4. Write down what you saw and felt in that earlier scene and compare it to your feelings and actions in the marital conflict.

Couple Sharing

1. Once you have both completed the first part of this activity on your own, pray for the Holy Spirit to lead you in sharing your images and experiences.

2. First, take turns sharing your images of your marital conflict and what you wrote down about how you perceived what you each felt in the conflict.

3. Remember the purpose of this activity is to grow in understanding and compassion.

4. Then each of you take turns sharing your experience of being emotionally wounded in childhood or adolescence.

5. Share how you felt in that situation when you were younger.

6. Describe to your spouse your understanding of how your core wounds play into your current marital conflict.

7. Listen to your spouse describe their core wounds and what they felt. Allow yourself to feel compassion for your spouse in the areas of their wounds.

8. Pray together and ask Jesus to heal you both from these core wounds and the wounds you have caused each other in your marriage as a result of your conflicts.

9

HEALING AND FORGIVENESS

*Be merciful, just as [also] your Father is
merciful.*
—Luke 6:36

As we discussed in the previous chapter, most conflicts in marriage
are *unresolvable* for one of two reasons. The first and most obvious
reason is that these conflicts reflect our intrinsic differences in personality, values, and lifestyle. No matter how hard we may try, we cannot
change our spouse or change ourselves to conform to our spouse's
expectations. Our attempts to do so violate their inherent dignity, as
well as our own, and thus injure both persons.

Unity can only be achieved through self-giving love. You will
grow in communion with your spouse only to the extent that you treat
each other with respect and with a genuine desire to establish cooperative teamwork. In the face of your many differences, teamwork
grows as you choose to submit your will to God's will and to blend
your differences through mutual submission. As we all know from experience, submitting our will can be very challenging. We inevitability
run up against our self-centeredness and unhealed emotional wounds.

This is the second and more troubling reason why many of our
conflicts remain unresolvable. Our wounded hearts and character
weaknesses make it extremely difficult to relate to each other lovingly, especially during intense conflict. These character weaknesses
reveal the areas where we have not yet matured in our capacity to
love. Similarly, our unhealed emotional wounds interfere with our

ability to trust love, even when it is offered freely and faithfully. After years of hurting each other and internalizing these hurts, we become like two porcupines trying to mate. Layers of self-protection block our capacity for vulnerability. Until we seek healing for these wounds, we can do little else than protect ourselves from further hurt while keeping a safe distance from the one to whom we pledged our wholehearted devotion.

Whether you are consciously aware of it or not, you and your spouse have had many experiences in your life where you were not treated with tender love and respect. Throughout your life, you haven't received the full nurturing and cherishing you need to thrive. In fact, at times you received just the opposite of nurturing love. This may have come in the form of rejection, violation, betrayal, or abandonment. Whether those deprivations of love occurred in childhood, in previous intimate relationships, or in your marriage with each other, they have affected you much more than you probably realize. These soul wounds have impaired your capacity to fully entrust your heart to your spouse. Sadly, some of your deepest wounds may have come from those closest to you, including your spouse, making it even more difficult to fully trust your heart to them. Your own actions and poor responses to these hurts have only made things worse.

Left to fester, emotional wounds can too easily become the breeding ground for bitterness and resentment. When we allow these resentments to build up, our hearts eventually become calloused and insensitive. We stop being kind, compassionate, and forgiving, as Christ is (see Eph 4:32). Instead, we treat each other with indifference or even disdain. Though we claim to be followers of Christ, we end up acting more like unbelievers, with our minds darkened and our hearts calloused (see Eph 4:17–19). Lies darken our minds. And our hearts become hardened when we don't face our hurts and deal with the accompanying anger in a constructive way. In rejecting his merciful and healing love, we give in to destructive patterns of relating.

This, I believe, is the concern St. Paul addresses in his letter to the church in Ephesus: "No foul language should come out of your mouth, but only such as is good for needed edification, that it may impart grace to those who hear. . . . All bitterness, fury, anger, shouting, and reviling must be removed from you, along with all malice" (Eph 4:29–31). These attitudes and behaviors—bitterness, fury, abusive anger, shouting, foul language, and reviling—are destructive in any relationship, but in marriage especially, they damage trust and hinder unity.

Destructive Attitudes and Behaviors

We can tell how much healing we need (from past and current wounds) by looking at the way we interact in the heat of our martial conflicts. Here are a few questions for you to consider in examining how you respond when in the heat of conflict with each other:

- Do you show honor and respect for each other, even when you are hurt and angry?
- Do your words and actions build each other up or tear each other down?
- Are you honest, or do you hide your thoughts and feelings?
- Do you say and do things that you later regret?
- Do you come away from your disagreements feeling closer or further apart?
- Do you leave the conflict encouraged or discouraged?

If you come away from your marital conflicts feeling disrespected, torn down, discouraged, and more distant, these are sure indicators that both you and your spouse need deeper emotional and spiritual healing. That shouldn't surprise you. In this fallen world, we all need more healing. Some of us need a considerable amount of healing before we can have the kind of intimacy and unity that we desire in our marriage.

In his research on marital dynamics, Gottman observed four common attitudes and behaviors that inevitably weaken and eventually destroy the bonds of love and unity in marriage. He observed that all the couples he studied exhibited these destructive patterns from time to time. However, when couples become chronically stuck in these patterns of dealing with conflict, it is a sign that their marriage is in distress and in need of immediate help.

These are the four destructive patterns that Gottman identifies:

- **Criticism:** a negative evaluation of the other person's character. Examples: accusations, name-calling, ridiculing, character assassination, blaming, judging.

- **Contempt:** a superior attitude filled with disgust; it is an attitude of looking down on and belittling your partner. Examples: mocking, eye-rolling, sarcasm, belittling comments, resentments, haughtiness.

- **Defensiveness:** a self-protective response to being on the receiving end of an attack. It escalates rather than resolves the conflict. Examples: denial, self-pity, whining, playing the victim, self-justifying behavior, ignoring, failing to acknowledge the complaint, walking away.

- **Stonewalling:** disengaging emotionally from conflict and constructing a fortress of self-protection around your heart. It usually develops over time, after the other three patterns have become entrenched. Examples: emotional disengagement, avoiding interaction, turning away in conflict, shutting down, falling out of love, silent treatments.[1]

These destructive patterns are evidence of our weaknesses in character as the result of our sin and self-centeredness. When we become aware of these destructive patterns in ourselves, we need to learn to humbly acknowledge our underlying attitudes and behaviors that contribute to them, and then repair the damage we've caused as quickly as possible with our spouse. This is the way to effectively restore trust (the subject of the next chapter). But in addition to addressing our actions and attitudes, we must also face the history of any unhealed emotional wounds that underlie these patterns and are exacerbated by them.

Our destructive actions and attitudes didn't just appear out of nowhere when we married. They are character weaknesses that have developed over a lifetime. They usually begin early in life in response to emotional hurts. Imagine a young child being criticized and belittled. He may not be able to defend himself in the moment, but he learns that criticism is a normal pattern of behavior, because it is modeled for him. Simultaneously, he develops a contemptuous attitude toward the one who hurts him and builds walls around his heart to protect against further assault. As he grows older, these behaviors come into play in his interactions with siblings and friends. When he later begins to date and form intimate relationships, these patterns of aggression and self-protection become even more entrenched. They have been cultivated by years of ignoring wounds and holding on to resentments. If these hurts in childhood, adolescence, and dating are severe enough, then the walls of self-protection become fortresses, blocking out love.

As I have noted throughout this book, we cannot heal our marital relationship without also healing these emotional wounds that we brought into marriage. Many of us have a hard time identifying and recognizing how our hearts were wounded. But we can perceive them by looking at our current unresolvable conflicts. Our wounds become most evident in those issues in marriage where we find ourselves overreacting in the heat of conflict.

Overreactions to Conflict

We are all familiar with situations in which we react irrationally to a situation of perceived hurt. Whether our reaction is fearful and withdrawing or angry and aggressive, it pulls us out of love and hinders our capacity to trust. Sometimes these reactions are obvious to those around us, but at other times these overreactions are hidden and internalized. In either case, we need to recognize that our reactions are stronger than the circumstance that set us off. Though it may feel like a life-and-death situation to us, it is rarely as critical as it feels in the moment.

Feeling overwhelmingly distressed, we act out during conflict and leave our spouse feeling demeaned or abandoned. As hard as it is for us to acknowledge, we end up wounding our spouse because we haven't faced our own suffering. Fr. Richard Rohr expresses this reality succinctly: "If you do not transform your pain, you will always transmit it."[2]

We will wound our spouse to the degree that we have not dealt with our unhealed emotional wounds. That is a sobering reality in marriage. In my relationship with Margie, we both overreacted in many kinds of situations. In each of these, without intending to, we hurt each other in the process. I mentioned a few in the last chapter, but those weren't the biggest issues in our marriage. The biggest and most painful issue that threatened our communion was my overreaction to her drinking and partying and our inability to meet each other in our underlying pain. My reactions to her drinking beer and partying with friends were much more extreme than what they should have been. Yet no matter how hard I tried to control my responses, I still reacted in ways that hurt us both.

Whenever Margie opened a beer or went out partying with her friends, the four destructive patterns—*criticism, contempt, defensiveness*, and *stonewalling*—were present in my mind and heart. Even though I rarely expressed my reactions out loud (after our first few years of marriage), Margie still felt their impact from my nonverbal responses. This is an area we struggled with for many years in our marriage and one of the contributing reasons we entertained thoughts of divorce in our early thirties.

This issue escalated a couple of years into our marriage, when I was in graduate school and our daughters were both under the age of three. Margie began partying with her friends as her primary form of recreation. From the beginning, I told her that I didn't like it and wanted her to stop. I thought the problem was all hers. We both had family members who were addicted to drugs and alcohol, so it was a red-flag issue for me, but I didn't understand why I was reacting so intensely. When she didn't heed my concern, I became inwardly angry and tried harder to get her to stop, but nothing I said seemed to make any difference. She only left our arguments feeling condemned and as if I was trying to control her behavior (which was true). My attempts to change her behavior only made things worse. Realizing I wasn't getting anywhere, I gave up trying to tell her how I felt and what I needed. Instead, I bottled up my anger. Over time, my resentment grew, and eventually my feelings of helplessness turned into resignation in this area of our relationship.

Without being fully conscious of it, I began demonstrating the four destructive attitudes and behaviors when I interacted with her about this issue. I formed judgments about Margie's character and began to see her through the filters of my negative perceptions of her when she was drinking (*criticism*). Before long, I began to act self-righteously and resentfully toward her whenever this conflict came up (*contempt*). Whenever she would try to address my actions, I would justify and defend myself and then walk away (*defensiveness*). Eventually, my responses led to withdrawal and silent treatments, and walling off my heart (*stonewalling*).

In the middle of one of these conflicts about four years into our marriage, I remember thinking to myself, "I am falling out of love." And yet at no time throughout all of it did I stop to consider that this might be a reactive issue in my life because of my childhood wounds (due to my dad's addiction to alcohol and my brother's drug addiction). I was convinced that Margie was the problem (because of her family history of addiction) and all I needed to do was to get her to change her behavior and everything would be better. It wasn't until after our marital crisis and my subsequent encounter with the Holy Spirit that I began to see that I had childhood wounds that contributed greatly to these conflicts.

Childhood Wounds

It seems obvious to me now, but until my midthirties I was almost completely unaware that I had any unhealed wounds that were affecting our marriage. (I should have known better since I was a therapist, but I now realize it was an area in which I remained in denial to protect myself from intense pain.) Specifically, I had no idea how strongly connected my reaction to Margie's drinking was to my feelings of fear and abandonment with my dad and brother Dave due to their addictions to alcohol and drugs.

Just the sight of Margie opening a beer triggered painful feelings of rejection, abandonment, powerlessness, and fear. To me, on an unconscious level, drinking meant *traumatic loss*, because my dad left when I was thirteen and I attributed his leaving to drinking. It also meant *unfaithfulness and betrayal*, because my dad was unfaithful to my mom when he was intoxicated. This connection between drinking and the fear of unfaithfulness was reinforced by my own behavior in high school. I found myself being extra-amorous with girls (in high school) when I drank too much.

Without knowing it, I was projecting all these sources of unresolved pain and anxiety onto Margie each time she drank. There is a sad irony in all of this. For Margie, drinking had a very different connotation. But it would take me many years to understand that her affection for drinking was rooted in very positive memories of her father. Though her dad was not ordinarily affectionate with her throughout her childhood, the one major exception was when he had something to drink after coming home from work each day. Every evening, he would sit under a big shade tree in his backyard and open a Budweiser. It was such a part of his life, everyone called him "Bud." Because he was more affectionate and approachable after a few beers, these were some of Margie's favorite memories with her father. (Is it surprising that Margie's favorite beer was also Budweiser?)

Margie and I had two completely different responses to our fathers' drinking. For Margie, with her "life-of-the-party" personality and warm experiences with her dad, drinking was a way of having fun, getting close, and being affectionate. This was the association she carried unconsciously into our marriage. Unlike me, she had not been wounded by her father's drinking. In fact, she felt more loved by her dad when he had a few beers. She couldn't understand why I was threatened by her drinking and why I didn't grab a beer and sit down under a shade tree and become more affectionate with her. Instead, I did just the opposite, which left her feeling rejected and alone. This tapped into her wounds from her father when he wasn't drinking.

I too felt rejected and abandoned each time she drank. In my mind, she may as well have been spitting in my face. I felt dishonored and betrayed. An inner alarm would go off inside me. It felt like a major threat to my survival. Deep down, without realizing it, I was afraid she would be unfaithful and leave me when she drank at parties with her friends. It was only in walking through my healing process that I was able to see these triggers and begin to uproot the deadly wounds from my heart.

I offer all this as a way for you to carefully reflect on areas of overreaction in your relationship and how these are connected to your emotional wounds. Take a moment to consider how these over-reactions are rooted in childhood wounds and have consequently manifested in your relationship with each other.

Take a Moment

1. Which of the four destructive patterns (criticism, contempt, de-fensiveness, and stonewalling) are evident in you and your spouse during heated conflicts?

2. Can you identify the wounds underlying those issues when you overreact in conflict? (Ask the Holy Spirit to reveal these to you.)

3. Describe the unconscious associations you make in these areas of conflict. What do you believe causes you to react? What are you afraid will happen? What judgments have you made about your spouse?

Fearful Judgments

Do you see how your uncontrollable reactions to conflict are coming from your wounds? These wounds are further revealed by your fearful judgments. These negative beliefs about your spouse (which we all have) originate in your unresolved hurts, which may have occurred anywhere in life, beginning in childhood. They may have happened within your family or outside it, before marriage or after you were married. Some of these wounds may have been caused by your own actions and reactions.

Whatever the source of your emotional wounds, it is your reactions to them that makes all the difference in whether you will be controlled by them in the future. When we turn to God when we are offended, face the accompanying anger we feel, and immediately forgive as Jesus did on the Cross, we can be restored to wholeness rather quickly. But few of us have responded this way while being hurt, particularly when we were younger. Instead, we probably felt helpless and confused.

Rather than continue in the state of feeling powerless and afraid, we attempted to gain some power and control over situations that feel similar. To protect ourselves, we formed negative perceptions about the character of the person who hurt us. We also began to see ourselves and God in a negative light through these wounding experiences. Keeping our pain buried beneath these judgments, our smoldering anger turned into bitterness and resentment, which continues to contaminate all our relationships. This is what the author of the letter to the Hebrews warns against: "See to it that no one be deprived of the grace of God, that no bitter root spring up and cause trouble, through which many may become defiled" (Heb 12:15).

Our deeply rooted bitterness and fearful judgments defile us and the people in intimate relationship with us, especially our spouse. These *fearful judgments* are the underlying cause of our overreactions. This is important for each of us to recognize. *Our spouse does not cause us to react the way we do.* Our own judgments and fears formed in our deepest hurts are the real culprits. To blame our spouse for our reactions is simply another form of defensiveness and a failure to take personal responsibility for our actions and reactions.

It took me a long time to recognize this dynamic in my relationship with Margie. While she was responsible for her behavior, I was responsible for my reactions to her behavior and my own attitudes and actions. I couldn't change her behaviors, but I was the only one capable of dealing with my internal reactions, and the fearful judgments that fueled them. Coming to this realization was the beginning of my healing process. For too long, I blamed Margie for my feelings associated with her drinking and partying. But, after some Spirit-led soul searching, I finally realized she was not doing any of it intentionally to hurt me. She was simply living from her own perceptions of what she thought would make her happy. If she had been married to someone else who wasn't threatened by her drinking, that imaginary husband may have responded in a completely different way. I can imagine a scenario in which she could have married someone who loved to sit under a tree and drink a few beers with her like her father did or who loved to party like she did. In that case, it wouldn't have been a conflict for them the way it was for Margie and me. My *fearful judgments* made this a huge issue in our marriage. I continued holding on to these negative perceptions of Margie, which kept me holding on to fear, bitterness, and unforgiveness.

To heal these wounds, I needed to forgive Margie as well as myself. I also needed to face the bitter roots of these judgments, which came originally from the hurts I experienced in my relationship with my dad and my brother. Once I actively renounced these fearful judgments I held toward each of them, I could forgive them. I also faced and released the pain and anger that was hiding behind the walls of my heart. All this came about as I entered more fully into a process of healing and forgiveness.

Forgiveness and Healing

In his book *Forgiveness*, Fr. Richard McAlear explains why forgiveness is essential for our healing:

> Forgiveness is very much a part of healing. . . . If we
> do not forgive, we cannot be forgiven; we block the
> movement of grace. Unforgiveness has two significant

effects. One is that it blocks the flow of healing. If
there is resentment, bitterness, and unresolved anger
in my spirit, it clogs the spiritual arteries and healing
love cannot flow. It is like a spiritual stroke and it is
deadly. If there is unforgiveness in the heart or spirit,
then healing cannot penetrate. We must choose to forgive deeply if we are to experience the healing love
of God. Love and anger cannot occupy the same heart
space at the same time. It is like darkness and light,
one contradicts the other. The greatest blockage to
healing is unforgiveness. Forgiveness opens the door
to healing.[3]

These wise words express the core Gospel message. Jesus forgives
us and commands us to forgive from our hearts (see Mt 18:35). Forgiveness begins with our wills, but to be fully effective, it must reach
the depths of our hearts, where our hurt resides. Fr. McAlear further
explains, "If the hurt is deep, forgiveness has to go just as deep. It
must reach to the depth within where the pain is felt. We cannot carry
a deep hurt in our heart and simply offer a shallow forgiveness that is
glib and empty. That is not forgiveness but denial. To say that it does
not matter when it does is not truth. To forgive from the heart is lib-
erating. There is acknowledgment of the hurt, release and freedom."[4]
Forgiveness from the heart entails more than just saying "I forgive
you." To be fully effective, it must also deal with the trauma and all
the self-protective strategies that have formed around our hearts. This
involves renouncing our fearful judgments, releasing our pain and
anger, and letting go of any unhealthy attachments that keep us and
others from being free.[5]

I discovered the power of forgiving and being forgiven during
the darkest winter season of our marriage, after I began seeking God
more earnestly. I didn't realize that the lack of communion between
Margie and me, and my blocks with God, were due largely to these
areas of unforgiveness that remained hidden in my heart. The initial

grace to forgive from the depths of my heart came on a spiritual retreat weekend.

At the beginning of the retreat, I was encouraged to pray for two specific graces—one to be granted during the weekend and the other to be received after the weekend was over. I prayed to know God in a deeper way than I had ever known him before (during the retreat), and to love Margie more deeply when I returned home.

The first grace was answered through an amazing series of events that occurred throughout the weekend. It started after I went to Confession for the first time in years and received God's forgiveness for my sins, and afterward experienced his healing presence in the Eucharist. Later that night, I encountered the Father's love during an intensely powerful prayer experience. The entire next day, I cried tears of joy as I released years of bottled-up pain.

I didn't realize the impact this release would have on my marriage until I went home and experienced the second answer to my prayers. When I saw my wife and children, I did so with new eyes, loving them with a renewed heart. As I embraced Margie, I began to cry tears of sorrow and joy. My heart felt alive, and I felt a deep love for her and was able to forgive her from my heart. Rather than holding on to my fearful judgments of her in that moment, I felt a new level of trust and compassion for her. After that healing experience, divorce was never again an issue in our marriage. That weekend was a pure gift of God's mercy and healing. It was my first breakthrough in heartfelt forgiveness.

Three months later, I experienced another breakthrough of divine healing and forgiveness. This time it was with my father. I was finally able to let go of the deep well of abandonment pain and betrayal that I felt with my dad leaving. Releasing this gut-wrenching pain, I was able to forgive my father and love him freely again, like I had as a child. That began a process of reconciliation in my relationship with him, which eventually spread to our entire family. A few years later, I was also able to forgive my brother Dave for the pain he caused our family from the ways he coped with his addictions. Since then, forgiveness has become a way of life and a regular part of my daily prayer. I have come to realize that this is the normal Christian life that the Church calls each of us to every day. Remember the phrase from the Our Father? "Forgive us our sins for we ourselves forgive everyone in debt to us" (Lk 11:3–4).

We know we have forgiven from the heart when we feel compassion for the person who hurt us, seeing that they were acting out of their own emotional wounds and immaturity. We can also see the evidence in the way we argue with our spouse. Our destructive patterns of behavior give way to genuine love. Honor replaces criticism; kindness replaces contempt; healthy boundaries replace defensiveness; and vulnerability replaces stonewalling. This is how we are all called to love as followers of Christ: "Be kind to one another, compassionate, forgiving one another as God has forgiven you in Christ" (Eph 4:32). This is what it means to *be devoted*.

While the issues we are dealing with in marriage are ongoing, we need to forgive our spouse and seek God's mercy for our sins and wounds every day. In my marriage, though my spiritual renewal weekend gave me a fresh start, I continued to deal with judgments toward Margie and needed to practice forgiveness as a way of life. I learned from that experience that heartfelt forgiveness is an ongoing process, bringing us deeper and deeper healing.

The following reflection questions and couple activity are opportunities to bring healing to you, your spouse, and your marriage. The forgiveness exercise can bring about powerful changes in your heart and relationship, so I encourage you to allow enough time and prayer for this healing to reach the depths of your hearts.

Take a Moment

1. Do you agree that your spouse is not the primary cause of your reactions? What is?

2. How do our fearful judgments develop? Can you identify an example of a fearful judgment in your life?

3. Who else besides your spouse do you need to forgive and for what do you need to forgive them? What do you need to forgive your spouse for?

Activity for Couples:
Forgiveness Prayer; Letter Writing, and Sharing

Individual Prayer Experience: Forgiving Your Spouse[6]

1. Ask the Holy Spirit to show you the offense for which you need to forgive your spouse.

2. Picture your spouse in front of you and pay attention to what you are feeling (angry, sad, afraid, powerless, hurt, disgusted).

3. How did your spouse hurt you? How has it affected you, and how has it affected your relationship with your spouse?

4. Tell your spouse (in your mind) what they did to hurt you and how it has affected you. It is okay to feel angry and express it ("I felt unloved"; "I felt alone"; "I continue to have trouble trusting you").

5. Ask the Holy Spirit to reveal to you what you believe about yourself as an effect of this wounding experience (how you have internalized the hurt into your self-image).

6. Renounce the damaging beliefs about yourself. (For example: "I renounce the lie that I am not loved or cared for; I renounce the lie that it is all my fault; I renounce the lie that I am powerless and can't trust again.")

7. Ask the Holy Spirit to reveal the fearful judgments you hold toward your spouse as a result of how you were hurt.

8. Renounce these judgments. (For example: "In the name of Jesus, I renounce the judgment that my spouse is mean, unfaithful, stupid, careless, selfish.")

9. In your imagination, stand at the foot of the Cross with your spouse.

10. Ask Jesus to forgive you for these fearful judgments and to forgive your spouse for the ways they hurt you.

11. As you stand at the foot of the Cross in your imagination, turn to face your spouse. Verbally forgive him or her.

12. Ask Jesus to give you his compassion for your spouse.

13. Pray a blessing over your spouse: Ask God to bless your spouse in the opposite way that they hurt you. (For example: "Father, please bless my husband/wife. Help him/her to know he/she is forgiven and accepted. Help him/her to receive your love and be fully restored in his/her identity as your beloved son/daughter. Help him/her receive my love.")

14. Ask Jesus to seal this forgiveness with his precious blood and to heal any remaining wounds.

15. Thank him for his mercy and healing.

Write a Forgiveness Letter to Your Spouse

Write a letter to your spouse describing the steps you went through in prayer. Tell them about the hurt you felt, the fearful judgments you made, the beliefs about yourself you internalized. Then write out your forgiveness, describing the compassion you now feel for them, the blessing you spoke over them, and how your view of yourself has changed.

Read Your Letters to Each Other

Agree on a time and quiet space where you can read your letters of forgiveness to each other. Take turns. Read your letters slowly. This is a time to listen and understand, not to argue or go deeper in discussing the unresolved issues. Discipline yourself to listen. At the end, thank your spouse for their forgiveness and for their vulnerability in sharing their letter with you. You may want to then give your spouse the letter as a gift to them. As you finish, thank God for his mercy and healing.

10

RESTORING BROKEN TRUST

Confess your sins to one another and pray
for one another, that you may be healed.
—James 5:16

In the previous chapter, I spoke about forgiveness as the primary means for healing our relational wounds. As vital as it is, forgiveness is only part of the process of healing and reconciliation within marriage. Forgiveness opens our hearts to love again. But it does not, by itself, restore the trust that has been broken in the relationship. Full reconciliation requires several other steps that are essential for restoring trust. These include acknowledging our failures and offenses, overcoming the character weaknesses that underlie them, and asking for God's grace as we engage in the challenging work of restoring the areas where trust has been broken in the relationship. This is often the most difficult part of the healing process, because confronting our personal shortcomings requires humility.

I spent most of my professional career accompanying couples in the process of reconciliation. Most of these couples were able to restore trust and communion in their marriage; but some failed to reconcile. The key difference in those couples who reconciled was their humility and dependence on God. Those who humbled themselves and were open to the Holy Spirit were able to eventually find healing for their marriage. However, those who held on to pride and self-justification remained stuck in their distress. They continued to hold on to fearful judgments of their spouse. Some couldn't get past their own shame and self-hatred. As a result, they failed to overcome their wounds and restore love in their marital relationship. Some of those couples ended up divorcing, while others remained married without any real communion. As a result, they and their children suffered interminably.

With those couples who humbled themselves and depended on God's help, I witnessed miraculous interventions in seemingly hopeless and irretrievably broken marriages. Many times, I saw God restore marriages in which trust had been devastated by multiple and ongoing infidelities. With one couple, the Holy Spirit gave the wife a vision of her husband's conversion hours before she got the news of his repeated adultery. She was naturally devastated by the revelation of his unfaithfulness, but because she trusted what she received in the vision, she was able to forgive her husband and hold on to hope.

Her forgiveness opened her heart to love him unconditionally, which kept them together until he was ready to face his sins and repent of them. Eventually he was able to forgive himself and make a heartfelt apology for his offenses against God, his wife, their family, and himself. This couple now has a beautiful love between them, and the husband has come to love and trust God for the first time in his life. He is also devoted to his wife and children because of his wife's faithfulness and unconditional love. It was truly the mercy of God, working through his wife's kindness, that led him to repentance (see Rom 2:4).

In another couple, the betrayal was equally devastating. The husband was sent to jail for seven years after having sex with a minor while he was intoxicated. His wife and children were distraught. I can barely imagine the level of betrayal and anguish they experienced. But trusting in God's love and mercy for their husband and father, they dealt with their pain, forgave him, and continued to love him unconditionally. While he was in jail, he was able to forgive himself and fully repent of his sin. After years of healing and prayer, they have worked through the underlying issues to fully restore the trust in their marriage and family. This man and his wife now genuinely love and respect each other, and the children love and honor their father. As unbelievable as that may seem, I came away understanding "nothing will be impossible for God" (Lk 1:37).

In a third couple, the broken trust was not due to sexual infidelity but the feelings of betrayal and shame were still very painful. This time it was the wife who betrayed her husband's trust by charging tens of thousands of dollars on credit cards. The husband remained the sole wage earner so that his wife could stay at home and care for their children. When he found out about the credit card bills, he was devastated and furious. Even though the wife promised her husband she would never do it again, it happened several more times. The third time, she humbled herself and acknowledged she had a serious problem and went for professional help.

Though devastated and angry each time, the husband worked through his feelings of betrayal and eventually forgave his wife. He also worked long hours to pay off the credit card bills—providing her with a living representation of Christ's merciful love paying the full price of our debts on the Cross. Over time, this couple restored their broken trust.

These examples are not as unusual as you might think. I believe God is willing and ready to do the same for all couples, but not everyone is willing to humble themselves in the way these couples did. Sometimes it takes us being overwhelmed before we are willing to concede that we need God's help and the help of others. I could go on with several more amazing stories of God's miraculous interventions in the lives of married couples. But that would only reveal part of the picture. There are also several situations where couples did not reconcile. Some of these sad situations involve Christian couples who struggled to forgive and restore trust. As a result, they remained bound in patterns of mistrust and contempt. Unwilling to fully humble themselves before God, become honest, face their deep hurt, and then repair the damage that prevents them from restoring communion, they have not yet developed the character qualities necessary for restoring trust.

Character Builds Trust

While forgiveness is given as an unconditional gift, trust must be established over time. After significant breaches in the relationship, trust often takes a considerable amount of time and effort to be restored. This is because trust depends on character, and this must be tried and tested. For example, when a spouse lies to their partner, this creates a major stumbling block to restoring trust. Honesty, which is a fruit of humility, is one of the fundamental character traits that enables trust to be repaired. Couples cannot build trust without being honest with each other. And yet honesty also requires vulnerability, which is difficult to reestablish without a baseline of safety and trust in the relationship.

I came into my relationship with Margie with some significant trust issues. When we met, I had not yet faced the wounds or received the healing I needed from the betrayals I had experienced during those tumultuous early teenage years. Because of those past wounds of betrayal, I became especially reactive when it came to issues of honesty and faithfulness. It didn't help my insecurities when Margie lied to me about smoking while we were still dating. She knew I would be upset if I knew, so she hid it from me. When I found out, I was hurt and angry about the issue, but it was her lack of honesty that hurt me the most. It tapped right into my previous wounds.

When we finally worked through the issue to resolution, Margie apologized and I forgave her, but it would take a while to restore the trust between us. We were both able to express our perceptions of the situation, and Margie assured me that she would not hide something from me again. I also realized I had a part to play in her not being honest with me.

In our conversations about the incident, I discovered she was hesitant to tell me the truth because she feared my disapproval. I realized that if I wanted her to tell me things she knew would upset me, I first needed to take responsibility for my part in the situation. I had to learn to respond in ways that would provide her enough safety to be honest and vulnerable with me. I also needed to avoid falling into fearful judgments in response to her choosing to do things I didn't like. But it was only after my deeper healing that I was able to be merciful instead of condemning. Instead of criticizing her, I was able to respond with more kindness. Instead of judging her, I matured in my ability to show compassion. Instead of closing off and shutting down, I vulnerably shared my hurts and desires with her.

In summary, her lack of honesty and my reaction revealed where we both needed to mature in areas of our character weaknesses. Restoring trust is ultimately about overcoming these character weaknesses with God's grace through growth in virtue. St. Peter provides a good summary of the character qualities that are necessary for cultivating mature love: "For this very reason, make every effort to supplement your faith with virtue, virtue with knowledge, knowledge with self-control, self-control with endurance, endurance with devotion, devotion with mutual affection, mutual affection with love. If these are yours and increase in abundance, they will keep you from being idle or unfruitful in the knowledge of our Lord Jesus Christ" (2 Pt 1:5–8).

Notice St. Peter's emphasis on *devotion*. It is an essential dimension of Christlike character. More than anything else, it is *endurance with devotion* that enables us to become trustworthy in marriage. Developing Christlike character takes time and requires patience. We can't just will ourselves to become instantly mature. No matter how much we attempt to love each other well, we will continue to fail many times throughout our dating and married life, right up until one of us dies. That is why we need to be honest about our failures and patient with ourselves and each other when we confront these failures. This is all a part of maturing in love: "Love is patient, love is kind, . . . [love] is not pompous, . . . it does not rejoice over wrongdoing but rejoices with the truth" (1 Cor 13:4–6). Christlike character is expressed in devoted love and grows as we humbly and honestly acknowledge our sins and failures and ask for God's help.

Confessing Our Failures

In *The 4 Seasons of Marriage*, Gary Chapman emphasizes three essential steps in the process of reconciliation: (1) identifying our personal failures; (2) confessing and repenting of our sins; and (3) forgiving ourselves and our spouse. These steps are fundamental for restoring trust in every season of marriage, but especially critical during the fall and winter seasons of our relationship. Chapman notes, "Marriage is a two-way street. Neither of you is perfect, and each of you must deal with your own failures. The first step is to identify these failures and take responsibility for them."[1]

Step 2, he asserts, is to make a good confession and repent. "The word confession means 'to agree with.' Therefore, you are agreeing with God that you were wrong. You are agreeing that your behavior has caused pain to your spouse and has grieved God's heart. Repentance means 'to turn around and walk in the opposite direction.' By repenting of your failures and the hurt you caused your spouse, you are expressing to God your desire to behave differently in the future. You are asking for the power of the Holy Spirit to enable you to love your spouse as God intends."[2]

Step 3 involves asking for and offering forgiveness. "Remember forgiveness is not a feeling. It is a decision to lift the penalty for past failures and declare the spouse pardoned. . . . Forgiveness does not mean that you will never feel the pain that accompanies the memory. Forgiveness does mean that you will no longer hold that failure or hurt against your spouse. As 1 Corinthians 13:5 says, love 'keeps no record of wrongs.'"[3]

For Catholics and others from liturgical backgrounds, the process of reconciliation begins with the Sacrament of Reconciliation. Confession with a priest enables us to face our shame and guilt and to be honest about our sins in a safe environment where we can anticipate that our sins will be met with God's mercy and grace. Pope John Paul II speaks about how reconciling with God first sets in motion other reconciliations:

> It must be emphasized that the most precious result of
> the forgiveness obtained in the sacrament of penance
> consists in reconciliation with God, which takes place
> in the inmost heart of the son who was lost and is found

again, which every penitent is. But it has to be added that the reconciliation with God leads, as it were to other reconciliations which repair the breaches caused by sin. The forgiven penitent is reconciled with himself in his inmost being. He is reconciled with his brethren, whom he has in some way attacked and wounded. He is reconciled with the Church. He is reconciled with all creation. (*Reconciliatio et Paenitentia*, 31)

Notice that reconciliation begins with God, then with ourself, and then with the person we hurt by our actions—in this case, our spouse. All three parties have been wounded by our failure to love. We wound God's heart by our unloving thoughts and actions and by the ways we fail to love (if you have a hard time imagining God wounded, picture Jesus on the Cross). When we hurt God and others, we also hurt ourselves. We see this expressed in shame and character weaknesses. Finally, we need to face the fact that we have hurt our spouse and wounded their trust. Therefore, it is essential that reconciliation address all three parties. You cannot restore trust with your spouse if you don't forgive yourself and grow in virtue. And it's hard to truly trust yourself to act in a loving way unless you first trust and rely on God to give you the grace to love with his love.

I realize we are dealing with difficult issues here. Before looking at how to put this into practice, let's pause a moment to reflect on and apply these understandings in your marriage.

Take a Moment

1. In which direction are you more likely to exhibit pride—judging your spouse for their failures or condemning yourself for your failures?

2. Review the three steps to reconciliation in marriage identified by Chapman. Which of these steps is most difficult for you? Why?

3. Why do you think it is important to confess our sins and failures to God, to the Church, and to our spouse?

A Good Confession

When we were young children and relatively innocent, many of us who were raised in the Church were taught how to make a good Confession. If that is your experience, do you remember the parts of a good Confession that you learned? It probably went something like this:

1. Prepare your heart by asking the Holy Spirit to show you what you need to confess.

2. Approach the Confession with sincere sorrow for hurting God, yourself, and others.

3. Confess specifically, with humility and honesty, what you did wrong.

4. Be ready to repair the damage and grow in maturity in that area of weakness in character.

5. Desire to do God's will in that specific area of weakness and all areas of your life.

These same principles for a good sacramental Confession also apply to apologizing to our spouse in marriage. Yet it seems much more difficult for many of us to make a good apology (a form of Confession) to our spouse. Is that because we anticipate that our spouse will not be merciful, as God is merciful? Or because we know that they see our failures sometimes better than we do? In either case, it can be challenging to know where to begin when it comes to confessing our failures to our spouse. It not only requires courage and humility but also know-how. Sometimes understanding how to make a good apology increases both our courage and humility.

Years ago, I attended mediation training from Ken Sande, a Christian attorney and the author of *The Peacemaker*. I was impressed with the thoroughness and effectiveness of his seven steps of a good apology. I recognized that if these steps were effective in his intense mediation work with couples, they might also be helpful in marriage counseling. So, I decided I would incorporate them into my work with couples. Over the years, I saw many couples benefit from applying these steps of apology. Since my retirement from private practice, I have presented these steps in helping couples reconcile during our Unveiled marriage conferences. I have heard many beautiful testimonies from those couples who have put these principles into practice.

I offer these as practical tools for you to apply in your marriage to restore trust in whatever way it has been damaged, whether the damage is major or minor. As you review these steps,[4] take them to heart. You will have an opportunity to put them into practice at the end of the chapter. Notice that each step is identified by a word beginning with the letter *A*. As you master them, you will become an "A" spouse. Read the steps slowly and reflect on each one.

1. **Address** directly the person(s) you offended.

2. **Avoid** excuses (no alibis, ifs, ands, or buts).

3. **Admit** both your wrong attitudes and behaviors.

4. **Acknowledge** the hurt of the person you wounded.

5. **Accept** the consequences of your behavior.

6. **Alter** your attitude and behavior (and be held accountable).

7. **Ask** for forgiveness: "Please forgive me when you are ready."

Let's examine these seven steps, one at a time, to see how you can apply them in restoring trust and reconciling wounds in your marriage.

Address Directly

The first step of a good apology involves addressing your spouse directly (and any other person you offended in the situation). This may seem obvious, but it needs to be stated, because many of us avoid facing our spouse and other people directly when we offend them.

This requires both humility and courage, so pray for those graces. It is humbling to face the ones we hurt and own up to our responsibility.

I have experienced the power of this in my family. About twenty-five years ago, my father (who died two weeks before Margie) entered a process of healing and reconciliation, first with God and then with our family. After attending a spiritual retreat weekend, he became active in Alcoholics Anonymous, where he worked through their renowned twelve-step program of recovery and became sober for the rest of his life. After facing and confessing his sins before God, he courageously wrote all of us a letter and took full responsibility for how he hurt us, in specific detail.

Later, he followed that up by addressing us face to face together as a family and then each of us individually. I was especially touched by his humility and honesty in apologizing to my mom. He did that once in front of all of us, but I also know from my mother that he apologized to her specifically and in person, on at least two other occasions, even though they had been divorced for many years by then. Watching my father humbly address his wrongdoings directly to my mom and each of us increased my admiration for him tremendously. Through it all, he didn't blame her once or make any excuses for his behavior.

Avoid Excuses

The second step in a good apology is avoiding excuses. I don't know about you, but I have a strong impulse to justify myself whenever I hurt someone or do something wrong. Rationally, I realize there is no need for me to justify myself, since Jesus has already justified me by his death on the Cross. But nevertheless, I fall back into self-justifying thoughts and behavior regularly, as part of my defensiveness. I want to explain away my actions. Even when I go to sacramental Confession, I must avoid the temptation to justify or excuse my sins in my own mind. Oftentimes, when I would apologize to Margie, it didn't feel clean because I would say things like, "I'm sorry for what I said, but I only said it because of what you did." (I know that wasn't very mature.)

By contrast, on those occasions when I took full responsibility for my actions, it felt good to be honest with no rationalizations or excuses. I can remember a time specifically when I came to her in humility and did not justify myself. I was watching a video on repentance, which addressed the sin of pride as a problem for many American men. In the middle of watching it, the Holy Spirit came upon me and convicted me of how my pride had hurt Margie and our children. I began to weep tears of contrition. I was able to apologize first to her and then to each of our daughters for the ways I hurt them by acting self-righteously. I could tell it touched them and restored their trust in me, especially as they saw me humbly admit my failures.

Admit Wrong Attitudes and Behaviors

The third step in a good apology is admitting that both our attitudes and behaviors were wrong and harmful. Have you noticed that when most of us admit we are wrong, we often stay at the surface of our actions without acknowledging the underlying attitudes behind them? Remember my story about Margie and me fighting over our housing situation (in chapter 6)? After we both surrendered the issue to God and began to have open conversations, I realized I had misjudged her motives. My attitude was arrogant, and I reacted stubbornly to her expressed desires for a new house. Fear was underlying both my arrogance and my stubbornness. I needed to apologize for my attitudes and actions. My apology went something like this (sitting face to face and looking her in the eyes): "Margie, I am sorry for the ways I hurt you these past several years about the house. I was wrong for being so stubborn. I realize it was prideful of me to think I knew what God wanted. And I was closed to listening to what you wanted or why you wanted it. I wrongly judged your motives. I am sorry."

Do you hear both my wrong actions and wrong attitudes? After admitting these wrongs, I then needed to listen to her express her hurt so I could understand her better and she could release her pain.

Acknowledge Hurts

The fourth step in a good apology is to acknowledge how you hurt your spouse. This involves listening to them express their pain. Sometimes when we apologize to our spouse, they will spontaneously start telling us how we hurt them. When Margie would do this after my apologies, I would become defensive at first and say, "I know I hurt you. That's why I'm apologizing." But I was still missing her heart. If our apology is sincere and humble, we must allow for our loved one to express their pain until it is released. Sometimes it comes out in anger, and that is okay too. When you write your letter to your spouse apologizing (at the end of this chapter), spend some time putting yourself in their shoes while trying to understand and feel their hurt.

Regarding the house situation, I might have said to Margie, "I realize it hurts you when I judge your motives and don't give you the chance to tell me why you want a new house. When I put myself in your shoes, I imagine it feels as though you don't have a voice and you feel frustrated that I won't even listen to you. I also can see how you would feel unloved and misunderstood because I haven't cared about your desires. Is that accurate?" Then she would have the opportunity to tell me directly how she felt. My role at that point was to be quiet, listen, and empathize, while doing my best to understand and put myself in her shoes. This is not always easy, but if we do it well, it can bring about considerable healing in the relationship. Acknowledging our spouse's hurt is just one of many ways of accepting the consequences that inevitably come from hurting them.

Accept Consequences

The fifth step of a good apology is accepting the consequences. Your thoughts and actions always have consequences, whether for good or evil. St. Paul offers some very sobering words of warning to all of us in this regard: "Make no mistake: God is not mocked; for a person will reap only what he sows" (Gal 6:7). We all have some level of self-deception when it comes to our sins and failures. We somehow act as though we can do whatever we want and there will be no consequences. But that is simply not reality. Everything we do has consequences. Have you ever heard the saying "Sow a thought and reap an action; sow an action and reap a habit; sow a habit and reap a character; sow a character and reap a destiny"? Every thought and action matters because everything we think, say, and do has consequences that affect our character and destiny, as well as those of the people around us.

I can't tell you the number of times I counseled couples dealing with a serious betrayal who didn't understand this part of the reconciliation process. Once the offended party is forgiven, they often act as though life should go back to normal. But they fail to see how much their actions damaged trust. This must be restored. And it takes time. The story of King David's adultery is a good example (see 2 Sm 11–12). As soon as King David confessed his sins, God forgave him. But God pointed out there would be consequences. Some of them were immediate and some lasted a long time. For example, David's entire family was affected for generations because of this and other sins. This may be an extreme example, but we all have stories like that.

Our behavior and our words have consequences for the people around us and for the generations that follow us. We need to accept these consequences. Sometimes this comes in the form of restitution, like the tax collector Zacchaeus. When Jesus invited himself over for dinner at his house, Zacchaeus spontaneously offered to make restitution for all his dishonesty and theft by repaying more than he stole (see Lk 19:1–10). This restitution was a visible indication he was accepting the consequences of his previous selfish and sinful behavior. It also showed he was intent on changing his attitude and behavior.

Alter Attitudes and Behaviors

The sixth step in a good apology involves making a firm decision to alter your attitudes and behaviors. This is true repentance. It is not enough to apologize and then go back to life as normal. This cavalier attitude only damages trust more. We need to make a commitment to change. But as we all know, there are things we think and do that are deeply ingrained and difficult to change, or they may have deeper roots than we realize. That is why repentance is a work of grace. It is not a do-it-yourself project. We always need God's help and often need the help of others. One well-known example of this involves overcoming addictions. I know many people who have tried to overcome addictions such as drugs or pornography, but they continue to fail until they actively seek God's assistance and the help of others in community. This is one of the gifts of the twelve-step programs. It emphasizes both our need for God and for others.

In marriage, when you apologize for something you did that hurt your spouse badly, there is a good chance this vice has deep roots in your life—in your thoughts and actions. You need to be serious about uprooting these vices before asking your spouse to forgive you. This will most likely involve getting help from someone you can trust, whether it is a friend, family member, professional, or a support group of some kind. As I look back over my life, most of my growth has come through Christian community, in church, men's groups, therapy, and spiritual direction. When we are intent on changing our behavior, we can then humbly ask for forgiveness.

Ask for Forgiveness

The seventh step of a good apology is asking for forgiveness. Notice it doesn't say *demand* forgiveness. Forgiveness is a gift that must be freely given and then freely received. It can't be demanded. Like every other expression of love, it must be given freely, fully, faithfully, and fruitfully. When you ask your spouse to forgive you, be humble and vulnerable. Understand this is not something you deserve or have earned. It is purely a gift of mercy. If your spouse is not ready, you can still receive God's forgiveness and forgive yourself. Do not allow your spouse's delay in forgiveness to keep you from doing the hard work of repentance.

If you are the spouse offering forgiveness, you might benefit from knowing the four promises of forgiveness Ken Sande identifies. In saying you forgive, you are promising your spouse that you (1) will not dwell on their past failures and weaknesses, (2) won't bring these failures up in arguments, (3) won't gossip to others about them, and

(4) will keep an open heart and a willingness to begin the process of restoring trust. At the same time, forgiving does not necessarily mean you will passively accept your spouse's abusive behavior. While you may need to forgive repeatedly, you don't have to be a victim in the relationship. You can choose how you will respond. Authentic love allows you to remain free in the Holy Spirit. Though always merciful, love cannot be manipulated. That is why, in addition to the seven A's, there is an important B-word that is essential for restoring trust: *boundaries*.

Establishing Healthy Boundaries

Boundaries are choices about how you will live your values and define yourself in relation to others. They are expressed in attitudes and behaviors that convey respect for God, yourself, and others. Contrary to popular practice, boundaries are not something we do to control our spouse's behavior. That would be manipulation and a violation of love. Rather, boundaries are things we do to change our own behaviors. It took me a while to learn this in my marriage.

Early in our marriage, when Margie did things I didn't like, such as smoking, I tried to convince her to stop doing it. When that didn't work, I took her cigarettes and threw them away. I thought this was setting a boundary, but instead it was a violation of her free will. She felt coerced by my attempts to change her. Later, I realized I needed to change my own behavior so I didn't violate her dignity but still honored my needs. So I expressed to her why her smoking bothered me (the effects on her health, my health, her example to the children, the children's health, the way she smelled when she smoked, and so on). Then I respected her freedom to resolve it.

By telling her how I felt about her smoking, and then by asking her not to smoke in the house, I was setting a healthy boundary. She respected my boundary by smoking on the porch. I would have preferred for her to quit smoking, but that was a choice only she could make. She in turn set a healthy boundary by letting me know I could not violate her free will. Her smoking on the porch was also a healthy boundary she set on her own behavior while still respecting some of my concerns.

Healthy boundaries define our relationship with others. They communicate what we are willing and unwilling to do. In marriage, we need to learn how to respect our self and our spouse. We can do this by clarifying how we will be treated and how we will treat our spouse. This is not always as easy as it sounds. Sometimes we need to grow in maturity and heal from our wounds before we can practice healthy boundaries consistently. If you want to learn more about this process of establishing healthy boundaries, I recommend a good book, *Boundaries in Marriage*, by Dr. Henry Cloud and Dr. John Townsend.[5]

The following discussion questions and couple activity are intended to help you understand the process of restoring trust through apology and repentance and to apply it in your marriage. At our Unveiled conferences, I have heard testimonies from many couples who have experienced major breakthroughs as they entered this process of apologizing and forgiving. I pray that you will also.

Take a Moment

1. Do you agree it is necessary to confess your failures to your spouse as well as to God? When would this not be beneficial or necessary?

2. Reflecting on each of the seven A's of a good apology, where do you see you need to grow in your character?

3. Suppose your spouse is verbally disrespectful toward you; what would be an example of a healthy boundary?

4. Are you willing to practice the seven A's in an apology letter to your spouse? If so, I encourage you to set aside some time and enter into the following activity prayerfully.

Activity for Couples: Apology Letter and Sharing

On Your Own

1. Begin in prayer, asking the Holy Spirit to show you how you have hurt your spouse and damaged trust between you in any area of your relationship. It may help to review the State of the Your Union Address from chapter 2 to reflect on the different areas of communion.

2. Be humble and honest with yourself before God. Write out all the ways you have failed to love your spouse well in those five areas of communion (spiritual, emotional, companionship, teamwork, and sexual), as well as the ways you have engaged in the four destructive patterns described in chapter 9 (criticism, contempt, defensiveness, and stonewalling).

3. Reflect on the damage and pain your attitudes and behaviors have caused your spouse, other members of the family, yourself, and God. How has this affected trust between you?

4. Now, slowly work through the seven A's as a way of preparing for writing a letter of apology to your spouse.

5. Write the letter addressing your spouse by going through the seven A's. Be careful to take full responsibility and be specific about the attitudes and behaviors that have been harmful. Don't forget to acknowledge your spouse's hurt and what you will do to change. Then ask for forgiveness at the end of the letter.

With Spouse

1. Agree on a time and place that is quiet and gives you enough time to share your letters with each other.

2. Slowly pray the Our Father together and invite the Holy Spirit to guide you.

3. Take turns reading your letters to each other.

4. Read slowly and pause after each section to give your spouse the opportunity to express their hurts.

5. Do not discuss the letters at this point. Simply read them and listen. When your spouse has finished, thank them for the gift they have given you in offering their apology. If you are ready to forgive them, say, "I forgive you." If you are not ready to forgive now, write them a letter later when you are ready and sit down and share it with them face to face.

6. After both of you have shared your letters, give them to each other so you can reflect on them later in solitude and prayer.

7. Offer a prayer of thanksgiving to God for your spouse and for the time you just shared together.

CONCLUSION

A LEGACY OF LOVE

Be imitators of God, as beloved children,
and live in love.
—Ephesians 5:1–2

Throughout this book, we have been learning about God's design for marriage as the blueprint for our happiness and fulfillment. From the beginning of creation, God destined us to experience communion with our spouse as an expression of our union with him. This is what we vowed when we married and what it means to *be devoted*. We spent the first part of the book (part I, "Becoming One") exploring how to develop communion in the five key areas of marital unity. I invited you to compose a State of Your Union Address, by examining how you and your spouse experience those five key areas of communion in your marriage. The reflection questions and couple activities were opportunities to grow in understanding and communion with each other.

Later, we noted how our human frailties—our sins, wounds, and self-centeredness—make it challenging to live God's intention out in practice. In part II, "Healing and Reconciliation," I proposed that every marriage needs healing from the wounds and sins we incur both before marriage and within the relationship. These wounds, sins, and character weaknesses are often most evident in our seemingly unresolvable marital conflicts. We discussed how understanding these conflicts will enable us to grow in unity and heal our underlying wounds. We then focused on how we can heal and restore trust through forgiveness, genuine apology, and growth in virtue.

If your marriage is anything like mine and Margie's, you realize that you still have a long way to go to live in the fullness of God's intention for your relationship. Every married couple faces obstacles that get in the way of loving each other well. As I shared throughout the book, I felt this gap acutely in my marriage with Margie at times. At other times, we experienced a taste of heaven when we loved each other well. You may also experience genuine love, but still know there is a gap between what you desire and how your marriage currently falls short of those desires. No matter how well or poorly you love your spouse and feel loved by them, you know you are created for so much more. This gap between our vows and our experiences directs us toward God as the source of our fulfillment. We live in hope to see his kingdom come "on earth as it is in heaven."

Jesus brought heaven to earth to reveal the merciful love of the Father. He walked the earth, taught about the kingdom of God, and healed infirmities to provide glimpses into the fulfilling life he desires for each one of us. Dying on the Cross, he broke the power of sin and showed us what true self-giving love looks like. After resurrecting from the dead, he gave us the sacraments of his love as the conduit through which we could have communion with him. These sacraments communicate the resurrection power of the Holy Spirit and are the source of our communion and healing with Jesus and one another.[1]

All the sacraments work in unison with the Sacrament of Matrimony, enabling us to heal and reconcile in the innumerable ways we have failed to give and receive love. They also provide the grace for us to love freely, fully, faithfully, and fruitfully. We are called to live in the fullness of love we promised each other when we spoke our sacred vows on the day of our wedding. In those vows, we promised to love each other as Christ loves us (see Eph 5:1b and 5:25). This fullness of love can be summarized in three simple but powerful words: *security*, *maturity*, and *purity*.

Security, Maturity, and Purity

Security is being *rooted and grounded in God's love* (see Eph 3:17). His love is the source of our love in marriage. Nothing else in life can provide that fundamental sense of trust and stability we each need to thrive. Following the example of Christ's covenant love, our sacred vows enable us to be devoted for life (chapter 1). They provide the spiritual glue that solidifies a secure bond between us. From this foundation of trust, we are then able to grow in unity in five key areas (chapter 2) through spiritual unity (chapter 3), emotional intimacy (chapter 4), daily companionship (chapter 5), cooperative teamwork (chapter 6), and sexual fulfillment (chapter 7). Each of these areas of communion helps to deepen our trust and unity in marriage while leading us into greater maturity.

Maturity is a process of *growing in Christlikeness* (see Eph 4:13). In doing so, we develop a greater capacity to love and forgive. As we mature in love, we simultaneously grow in all the virtues, helping ourselves and our spouse cultivate Christlike character (chapter 10). As we mature in love and the other virtues, we develop the capacity to submit ourselves to God and to each other, increasing our spiritual and emotional intimacy (chapters 3 and 4), setting our priorities in right order (chapter 5), and learning how to cooperate (chapter 6). This in turn helps us to give ourselves in lovemaking (chapter 7) and to deal with our conflicts in a mature manner (chapter 8).

Finally, maturity necessitates our dedication to ongoing healing and reconciliation (chapters 9 and 10). Deacon James Keating observes, "To 'suffer' the healing of your spouse is to endure his or her spiritual, moral, and emotional conversion by way of your grace and promised vowed love. The spiritual goal of Catholic marriage is to mediate grace from God for the mutual conversion of the spouses."[2] In other words, Catholic marriage is the vocation by which we encourage each other and our families on the path of holiness. This necessitates that each of us grow in purity.

In *purity*, we love each other as Christ loves us, with *complete self-giving* (see Eph 5:25). Purity is the natural outgrowth of security and maturity (Eph 5:1–4). In purity, we can see our spouse through the eyes of Christ and see God's goodness and beauty in them despite their human weaknesses. We do this as we overcome our fearful judgments and look at ourselves and our mates with compassion (chapter

9). This is how we overcome the obstacles and destructive patterns that weaken trust and hinder intimacy (chapter 8).

We cultivate purity as we invite the Holy Spirit into every area of our relationship, including lovemaking. Purity is the key to sexual fulfillment, as lust is transformed into pure love (chapter 7). Purity becomes evident outside the bedroom when we quit blaming our spouse for our overreactions and begin to understand and take responsibility for our part in martial conflicts (chapter 8). Purity increases as we heal our wounds and forgive each other for the ways they have hurt us (chapter 9). Purity also grows when we humble ourselves and apologize for the ways we caused harm to our spouse and then pledge to grow in holiness (chapter 10).

Growing in holiness is the challenge for every marriage. Every Christian marriage is meant to be a foretaste and sign of Christ's love for all eternity. Nothing else in marriage matters more than preparing each other for our ultimate wedding day with our eternal Bridegroom. I felt this reality profoundly when I handed Margie over to Jesus on the final day of our earthly marriage. A little more than a year after her death, on All Souls Day, I had what seemed like an inspired dream in which I received a package from heaven with writing on it. Immediately I recognized the handwriting as Margie's. Her words touched me deeply: "I am your greatest accomplishment on earth. Thank you for helping me get here (to heaven)."

As touched as I was by the message, I also wondered why the package was cut in half, since I only saw one half. As I prayed, I understood that the other half represented me. God gave us as a gift to each other. The picture will not be complete until I arrive with Margie in heaven and share in Jesus' glory with her, accompanied by all our loved ones. This is what I pray for each morning. I ask Jesus (with Margie's intercession) to prepare me and all our loved ones for the final wedding feast. This will be the final legacy of our marriage—a legacy of love.

A Legacy of Love

As you may have noticed throughout this book, I have said little about family life, because my focus has been primarily on marriage, which is the cornerstone of the family. As marriage goes, so goes the family (to a large extent). Our marriages exist first as witnesses to Christ's love in the Church and the world, then for our mutual benefit, and finally *for the benefit of our children and the generations to come.* This reality came home to me in a powerful way several years ago as God spoke to me through others about the graces our marriage brought to the generations of our family, despite all the struggles we had to overcome.

The prophetic messages were delivered on two separate occasions, by two different men. The first time, these inspired words were spoken to me alone. The second time, the message was given to my daughter Kristen while I was present. I believe God wanted to give us a glimpse of the many beautiful fruits of our marriage when we couldn't see it clearly because we were too immersed in the struggle.

This is a paraphrase of the first prophetic message that I received (God speaking through another person): "I want you to know that I see your faithfulness in your marriage in all that you have walked through. Because of all you have suffered in love, your children and grandchildren will walk in freedom and enjoy the fruits of all you have gained in intercession for them. They will all know me and love me. Their marriages and families will be blessed in ways beyond anything you have known in your childhood and in your marriage." As I heard these words, I knew they were from the Lord. Instantly I was moved to tears. But then as much as I was touched in the moment, later I doubted.

So God affirmed it again. This time, the message was directed to my daughter Kristen. This is a paraphrase of what I heard the second man proclaim to her: "Because of what your father walked through, trusting me and being faithful to what I have asked him to do, you and your sister and your family will stand on the shoulders of your parents' marriage. You will not have to struggle as they have in overcoming the issues they brought into their marriage. They have set a clear path for you and your family to walk on."

As I listened to these words of encouragement coming from the Holy Spirit through this man, I began to weep again. (I am weeping again writing them.) God was confirming my deepest desires. I have always desired a holy family dedicated to Christ. Margie and I were married at Holy Family Church, on the eve of the Feast of the Holy Family. Though we failed often to love each other in the way we promised in our wedding vows, Jesus continued to redeem our love. He took all our failures upon himself on the Cross and continues to transform them by his grace.

I believe those prophetic messages I received are not just for me and my family. They are for you and your family as well. The promises for your marriage are conditional, provided you continue to put into practice the truths you have learned throughout your life. This is the final message I want to leave with you. I know marriage can be difficult. I know what it's like to want to give up and find love somewhere else. But there is no other love apart from the love God ordains (see 1 Jn 4:7). On our wedding day, God gave us as a gift to love each other freely, fully, faithfully, and fruitfully "until death do we part."

Never give up! God's mercy is greater than any of your or your spouse's failures. God's grace is stronger than any of your character weaknesses. God's love is more bountiful than anything you long for or could possibly desire for your marriage. I believe with my whole heart that he desires to pour out his love into your marriage and to bless your family for generations to come. I know it's true. I've tasted it and watched many other couples experience the blessing of their marriage as they submit to each other out of reverence for Christ (see Eph 5:21).

In closing, I offer this blessing for you and your marriage (through a psalm of King David):

> Blessed are [you] who fear the Lord,
> and who walk in his ways. . . .
> Your wife will be like a fruitful vine

within your home,
Your children like young olive plants
    around your table.
Just so will [you] be blessed
    who fears the LORD.

May the LORD bless you . . .
    may you see Jerusalem's prosperity
    all the days of your life,
    and live to see your children's children. (Ps 128:1,
        3–6)

May you to continue to live out these blessings in your marriage, and may they increase and abound for generations to come. These final reflection questions along with the couple activity are intended to help you live out these blessings every day of your life.

Take a Moment

1. How would you assess your security, maturity, and purity as a married couple?
2. What is the legacy you want to leave for your children and grandchildren?
3. What changes are necessary in your life and marriage to leave such a legacy?

Activity for Couples: Be Devoted

Make a firm decision to *be devoted* to each other. A practical way to do this is to incorporate the various couple activities from throughout the book into your daily life (see appendix 1). If it feels overwhelming to do these all at once, add one practice a week until you have incorporated all of them. If your spouse is not motivated, you can still practice these activities yourself. Don't give in to excuses or rationalizations. Remember, this is the most important legacy you can leave your children and grandchildren, and your choices have both temporal and eternal consequences.

1. Make a firm decision to be devoted to God and your spouse (Introduction).

2. Establish a special occasion to reaffirm your wedding vows ("Devoted for Life").

3. At the end of each month, review the State of Your Union by assessing how you are doing in the five key areas of communion ("Five Key Areas of Unity").

4. Pray together at a set time each day, inviting God's blessing and protection into your marriage, bringing all your concerns to the Father, and thanking him for all he has given ("Rooted in Christ: Spiritual Unity").

5. Practice being vulnerable and expressing empathy by sharing your joys and sorrows with each other at the end of each day ("Heart to Heart: Emotional Intimacy").

6. Plan daily, weekly, and yearly activities that you enjoy doing with each other—then follow through ("Hand in Hand: Daily Companionship").

7. Once a week, spend thirty minutes practicing mutual submission and enthusiastic agreement on a specific issue in your marriage ("Side by Side: Cooperative Teamwork").

8. When you express your love for each other in the marital embrace, pray together first and then give yourself freely, fully, faithfully, and fruitfully, as a renewal of your wedding vows ("Body and Soul: Sexual Fulfillment").

9. When conflicts arise, pay attention to the difference between the content issue and the underlying relational issues ("Understanding the Roots of Conflicts").

10. Make a commitment to uproot the destructive relationship patterns in your marriage and practice forgiving your spouse every time you are offended ("Healing and Forgiveness").

11. Continue to humbly acknowledge your failures in loving each other. Apologize, make amends, and dedicate yourself to grow in Christlike character every day ("Restoring Broken Trust").

12. Keep your focus on the big picture. Grow in security, maturity, and purity. Leave a legacy of love for your children and grandchildren ("Conclusion: A Legacy of Love").

ACKNOWLEDGMENTS

Throughout my life, I have been blessed by devoted love. Though imperfect and at times distorted, I have never doubted the love of my family, friends, my heavenly Father, and the Communion of Saints that surround me. I am grateful for each of you.

Thank you, Father, Jesus, and Holy Spirit, for literally everything, and especially for revealing the essence of devoted love.

Thank you, St. John Paul II, for expanding our vision of marriage and family life so we could glimpse the beauty and majesty of God's design for the Sacrament of Matrimony.

Thank you, Christopher West and all those at the Theology of the Body Institute, for your dedication and passion in making John Paul II's teaching accessible to so many.

Thank you, Mom and Dad, for your love for me and our family. Though your marriage was eventually broken, you continued to affirm what the Church taught about marriage. Your teaching and early example were my first inspirations.

Thank you to each member of my extended family, brothers and sisters, nieces and nephews, aunts and uncles, and grandparents for your love and support. You have enriched my life and love for family.

Thank you, Fr. Richard Knuge. The course you taught at Chaminade High School first stirred my passion for studying the Christian vision related to marriage, family, and psychology.

Thank you to all my professors at Florida State University and my fellow graduate students who shared my passion for studying marriage and family life. You helped open my understanding.

Thank you, Bill and Pat Beckett, for introducing us to Marriage Encounter, and for helping me with my research on marital enrichment.

Thank you, Jim and Lois Galbraith, for showing me and our community the beauty of devoted marital love. Thank you for love and friendship, for reviewing this manuscript, and always encouraging me in my writing.

Thank you, Greg and Julie Alexander, Jeannie and Bruce Hannemann, Greg and Stephanie Schlueter, Paul and Gretchen George, and Ryan and Mary-Rose Verret for your lifelong dedication to building and restoring holy marriages. I appreciate each of you for your willingness to review this book and to be witnesses to the reality I tried to communicate.

Thank you, Gregory Popcak, Willard Harley, and Gary Chapman, for your wisdom and research on marriage and your lifelong dedication to ministering to married couples. I quoted you often throughout this book, because you have intimately walked with married couples and know what makes a difference.

Thank you, Sr. Miriam James Heidland, Fr. Tom Dillon, Fr. John Burns, Candace Ochoa, Tori Vissat, Kelly Mullins, Mike and Terese Jensen, Nicole and Lance Rodriguez, Sayli and Steven Samol, Christopher and Stephanie Lafitte, Peggy Schuchts (Mom), and Kathy Tafuri, for reviewing this book at different stages. I appreciate your honesty and encouragement, and more than that, your love and friendship.

Thank you to all our team at the John Paul II Healing Center: Judy Bailey, Kim Glass, Kristen Blake, Maria Botero, Bart Schuchts, Ken Kniepmann, Sr. Miriam James Heidland, Carrie Daunt, Duane Daunt, Alane Howard, Melissa Perez, Nicole Rodriguez, and Colleen Nixon. I love sharing this mission with you. You are each passionately devoted to loving Christ and serving his Bride, the Church.

Thank you to our board members and all of our Friends of JPII. You have a share in this book because of the ways you support this mission. I appreciate your dedication to bringing about transformation in the heart of the Church.

Thank you to my treasured family for all your love and support. You are a witness to enduring love for me and for many others. Particularly, thank you, Stephen and Kristen, Carrie and Duane, for living the truths contained in this book. I love you very much.

Thank you, Anna, Drew, Ryan, Jack, Luke, Lily, Elle, and Will (our grandchildren). You each bring so much joy and fulfillment to me and to all of us. You are the fruit of your parents' devoted love, and I know that you will live it faithfully in the next generation. I love and delight in you.

Finally, thank you to all the devoted staff at Ave Maria Press and especially to Kristi McDonald, my editor. Kristi, it is a joy to share this work with you. Thank you for your passion for this project from the start and for all the extra work you put in to get it moving—helping me get past my writer's block, your helpful insights, serving as my liaison with Ave, and bringing this book to completion.

DAILY EXAMINATION AS A COUPLE

Covenant: Did we love, honor, and cherish each other today? Were we faithful and true to each other in thought, words, and actions?

Spiritual Unity: Were we in spiritual unity today? Did we pray together and for each other during the day? Was Christ at the center of our marriage today?

Emotional Intimacy: Did we feel emotionally connected today? Did we recognize and share our emotions where appropriate, with love?

Companionship: Did we enjoy spending time together today with each other? What did we do together that was enjoyable and nourishing?

Teamwork: How well did we cooperate today as a couple? Did we consider each other's interest and mutually submit to each other in our decision-making?

Physical Affection: Have we felt physically, emotionally, and spiritually connected today, through gaze, touch, hugging, or sexual intimacy?

Healing and Reconciliation: Did we resolve any issues between us today? Are we at true peace with each other as we go to sleep?

Special Attention: What area of our relationship needs our special attention today? What will we do tomorrow to make it better?

PRAYERS FOR FOSTERING UNITY

Releasing Unhealthy Attachment with Parents

Heavenly Father, I acknowledge that I have not fully left my parents to be joined to my spouse. I now renounce any unhealthy attachment I have with either of my parents. I release them to you, Father, and I ask you to give them the grace to release me. I declare that my primary allegiance is to you and to my spouse. I pray this in the name of the Father, Son, and Holy Spirit. Amen.

Releasing Unhealthy Attachment with Children

Heavenly Father, I recognize that I have formed unhealthy attachments with my children, and that this is unhealthy for their growth and development and for my relationship with my spouse. I ask you for the grace to release those unhealthy attachments now, and to form a healthy bond with my spouse, in the name of the Father, Son, and Holy Spirit. Amen.

Renouncing Unholy Soul Ties

Father, I ask your forgiveness for my unholy relationship with_____(name) in the past or present. (If you don't know a person's name, then offer the person without a name.) I renounce any unholy bond—mentally, emotionally, physically, sexually, or spiritually—that I formed with that person. I now formally break and cut these ties and offer this person to you. In the name of the Father, Son, and Holy Spirit. Amen.

Prayer to Be a Better Husband

Lord, I admit that I am inadequate to love my wife without your help. I ask for your grace to be perfected in my weakness, so I can give myself freely, fully, faithfully, and fruitfully to my wife, and nourish and cherish her as the gift she is to me. Lord, help me to be receptive to your covenant with me, so I can remember my sacred covenant vows to my wife. Thank you for hearing my prayers. Amen.

Prayer to Be a Better Wife

Lord, I admit that when I close my heart in self-protection and seek false outward forms of attractiveness, I lose my true inner beauty and my ability to be who you called me to be. I ask for your grace to be restored in my true nature and beauty, be receptive to my husband, and nurture our communion with tenderness and trust. Help me to always live out my calling to foster communion in our marriage. Assist me to love my husband freely, fully, faithfully, and fruitfully. Thank you for hearing my prayers. Amen.

Prayer of Blessing of Spouse

Heavenly Father, you are the source of all goodness and blessing. Please pour out your love and blessing on my (husband/wife) today and fill (him/her) with a knowledge of your love and (his/her) own goodness. I ask for a special blessing in this area of my (husband's/ wife's) specific need today (name specific need_____). Thank you for hearing my prayer.

Prayer for Spiritual Unity as a Couple

Heavenly Father, help us become one in Christ, through the power of your Holy Spirit. May your kingdom come, and may your will be done in every area of our marriage, as it is in heaven.

Prayer for Teamwork

Heavenly Father, I surrender my will to you. Help me submit myself to you and to my spouse out of reverence for Christ. Help me to look out for my (husband's/wife's) interest as well as my own. Reveal your will to us. Enable us to reach an enthusiastic agreement, with you and with each other. I ask this in Jesus' holy name. Amen.

Prayer before Lovemaking

Heavenly Father, thank you for the gift of my (husband/wife). Please bless and protect each of us body, soul, and spirit so we can give ourselves freely, fully, faithfully, and fruitfully to each other. I ask you to send your Holy Spirit so we can love each other deeply and from a pure heart, with joy, peace, passion, gentleness, generosity, and self-control.

Prayer in Midst of Conflict

Heavenly Father, thank you for making us different—including how we see things differently. Please help us reverence and understand each other in our differences and maintain a soft and tender heart even when we are in the midst of conflict.

Prayer for Forgiveness

Merciful Father, I ask you to forgive me for the ways I have offended you and my spouse. Please give me the grace to forgive my (husband/ wife) as you have forgiven me.

Prayer for Releasing Fearful Judgments

Merciful Father, help me let go of my fearful judgments and see my (husband/wife) as you see (him/her), in wholeness and with love and truth. In the holy name of Jesus, I now renounce this fearful judgment (state the judgment (_____) toward my (husband/ wife) and forgive him/her for hurting me. Holy Spirit, I ask you to show me where my judgments are rooted in my fears and insecurity (spend time listening in prayer).

Prayer for Restoring Trust

Merciful Father, I realize that every time I hurt my (husband/wife) I am wounding Christ. I ask for the grace of humility so I can see my own faults, take full responsibility for my actions, humbly apologize, and remedy the situation, so that our peace and trust can be restored.

Prayer for Generational Blessing

Good and Gracious Father, you promise to bless those who love you for a thousand generations. I ask now for the ability to live in communion with you, in every area of my life, and most especially in our marriage. I ask you to bless our love so that the generations to follow will grow up in a legacy of faith, hope, and love. Thank you for your goodness toward us. Amen.

RESOURCES FOR HEALING

If you have completed this book, you probably have a greater awareness of your need for healing, individually and as a couple. The following resources to support your personal and marital healing are available on the website of the John Paul II Healing Center (www.jpiihealingcenter.org).

Conferences

You can choose from a variety of healing and equipping conferences. Unveiled is the marriage conference that parallels the material in this book. It provides healing and intimacy-building experiences that cannot be fully communicated in a book. If it is not currently listed on the website, you can check on future conferences through emailing us at info@jpiihealingcenter.org.

There are several other conferences you may want to explore. The five-day conferences (Healing the Whole Person, Holy Desire, and Restoring the Glory) provide opportunities for in-depth healing. The two- or three-day conferences provide many opportunities for healing and equipping. There are also individual conferences for men (Men on Fire) and women (Undone).

Talks and Workbooks

If you are not able to attend a conference, you can listen to the teaching and personally work through the workbook material, individually or as a community. Introductions to different talks are available in the store section so you can discern which talks would be best. Sets include: Unveiled; Ablaze; Healing the Whole Person; Restoring the Glory; Holy Desire; and Real Suffering (which includes a book, journal, video series, and leaders guide).

Books

Be Healed; Be Transformed; Loved as I Am; Lenten Healing; Undone; Real Suffering; and *She Called My Name.* Descriptions of each are on the website.

NOTES

Introduction

1. I will unfold the process of this transformation and healing in our marriage throughout the rest of the chapters. See chapter 1 of my book *Be Healed: A Guide to Encountering the Love of Jesus in Your Life* (Notre Dame, IN: Ave Maria Press, 2014) for an overview of my healing process.

2. *Merriam-Webster*, s.v. "devote (*v.*)," accessed September 16, 2019, merriam-webster.com/dictionary/devote.

3. Dictionary.com, s.v. "devote (*v.*)," accessed September 16, 2019, dictionary.com/browse/devote.

4. *The Order of Celebrating Matrimony*, 2nd edition (Totowa, NJ: Catholic Book Publishing Corp., 2016).

5. *The Order of Celebrating Matrimony*, 2nd edition, 2016.

1. Devoted for Life

1. The wording is taken from the most up-to-date version of *The Order of Celebrating Matrimony*, 2nd edition, 2016.

2. I first heard these four characteristics of love from Christopher West. The core teaching is in the writings of John Paul II, *Familiaris Consortio* (*The Role of the Christian Family in the Modern World*), 11–22.

3. Julián Carrón, *Disarming Beauty: Essays on Faith, Truth, and Freedom* (Notre Dame, IN: University of Notre Dame Press, 2017).

4. Cormac Burke, "Annulments: The Good of the Spouses, of the Family, and of the Church," *Linacre Quarterly* 67, 2000 no. 3 (August): http://www.cormacburke.or.ke/node/308.

5. I strongly recommend that you pray through these attachments by "breaking unholy soul ties." Among the most important attachments that must be released are those originating in previous sexual relationships—in fact or fantasy.

6. See appendix 2 for prayers for releasing these attachments.

7. *Code of Canon Law*, Canon 1055: "The matrimonial covenant, by which a man and a woman establish between themselves a partnership of the whole of life, is by its nature ordered to the good of the spouses and to the procreation and education of offspring."

8. James Keating, *Spousal Prayer: A Way to Marital Happiness* (Omaha, NE: Institute for Priestly Formation Press, 2013), 10.

2. Five Key Areas of Unity

1. John Paul II, *Man and Woman He Created Them: A Theology of the Body* (Boston: Pauline Books and Media, 2006), 9:2–3.

2. Christopher West, *Fill These Hearts: God, Sex and the Universal Longing* (New York: Image Books, 2013).

3. The Church grants declarations of nullity for couples who have married in the Church but fail to establish true covenant with each other. Their marriage is not a valid sacrament because they did not have proper intentions.

4. Albert Mehrabian, *Silent Messages: Implicit Communication of Emotions and Attitudes* (Belmont, CA: Wadsworth Publishing, 1971). He estimates that 7 percent of any message is conveyed through words, 38 percent through tone of voice, and 55 percent through facial expressions, gestures, posture, etc.

5. John Gottman, *The Seven Principles for Making Marriage Work: A Practical Guide from the Country's Foremost Relationship Expert* (New York: Crown, 1999), 6–7.

3. Rooted in Christ: Spiritual Unity

1. Tertullian, *Ad uxorem*, 2:8, 6–8: CCL, 1, 393; cited by John Paul II in *Familiaris Consortio*, 13.

2. Squire Rushnell and Louise DuArt, *Couples Who Pray: The Most Intimate Act Between a Man and a Woman* (Nashville, TN: Thomas Nelson, 2011). Gregory Popcak, *How to Heal Your Marriage and Nurture Lasting Love: When Divorce Is Not an Option* (Manchester, NH: Sophia Institute Press, 2014), 105.

3. Ann Voskamp, *One Thousand Gifts: A Dare to Live Fully Right Where You Are* (Grand Rapids, MI: Zondervan, 2011), 205.

4. Keating, *Spousal Love*, 7.

5. Keating, *Spousal Love*, 8.

6. Keating, *Spousal Love*, 7.

7. Voskamp, *One Thousand Gifts*, 193.

8. St. Ignatius of Loyola in his twelfth rule of spiritual discernment says that the enemy is like a commander of an army looking for our areas of greatest weakness, so that he can attack us and conquer us.

9. See *CCC* 2766; Gerhard Lohfink, *The Our Father: A New Reading* (Collegeville, MN: Liturgical Press, 2019).

4. Heart to Heart: Emotional Intimacy

1. See Gregory Popcak, *Exceptional Seven Percent: The Nine Secrets of the World's Happiest Couples* (New York: Citadel Press Books, 2000).

2. See Gottman, *Seven Principles of Making Marriage Work*, 6; Willard F. Harley Jr., *His Needs, Her Needs: Building an Affair-Proof Marriage* (Grand Rapids, MI: Revell, 1986).

3. Harley, *His Needs, Her Needs*.

4. Gottman, *Seven Principles of Making Marriage Work*.

5. Gary Chapman, *The 4 Seasons of Marriage* (Carol Stream, IL: Tyndale House, 2006).

6. Chad Ripperger, *Introduction to the Science of Mental Health*, 3rd ed. (Sensus Traditionis Press, 2013), 133–170.

7. Jay Stringer, *Unwanted: How Sexual Brokenness Reveals Our Way to Healing* (Colorado Springs, CO: NavPress, 2018), 193–202.

8. See Gottman, *Seven Principles of Making Marriage Work*, 31–48.

5. Hand in Hand: Daily Companionship

1. See John Paul II, *Man and Woman He Created Them*, 5–7.

2. See Dennis Linn, Sheila Fabricant Linn, and Matthew Linn, *Belonging: Bonds of Healing and Recovery* (Mahwah, NJ: Paulist Press, 1992); Harley, *His Needs, Her Needs*.

3. Popcak, *How to Heal Your Marriage*, 88.

4. James G. Friesen, E. James Wilder et al., *The Life Model: Living from the Heart Jesus Gave You* (Lexington, KY: Shepherd's House, 2000), 61–62.

5. Jimmy Evans, *Marriage on the Rock: God's Design for Your Dream Marriage* (Dallas, TX: Marriage Today, 2005), 29.

6. *Cursillo* is a Catholic spiritual retreat weekend aimed at living our faith in Christ as the center of our lives.

7. Popcak, *How to Heal Your Marriage*, 85, 88.

6. Side by Side: Cooperative Teamwork

1. I tell the story about my brother Dave in *Be Healed* and *Real Suffering*.

2. Willard F. Harley Jr., *Give and Take: The Secret to Marital Compatibility* (Grand Rapids, MI: Revell, 1996). In a later book, *He Wins, She Wins*, Harley describes how to address the most challenging areas of marriage, including finances, child-rearing, sexual intimacy, time management, family

and friends, spiritual unity and emotional intimacy, all through this process of enthusiastic agreement.

7. Body and Soul: Sexual Fulfillment

1. John Paul II, *Man and Woman He Created Them*, 109:2.

2. John Paul II, *Man and Woman He Created Them*, 17:3.

3. Christopher West, *Heaven's Song: Sexual Love as It Was Made to Be* (West Chester, PA: Ascension Press, 2008), 67. West was citing Theology of the Body, 111:1.

4. Christopher McCluskey and Rachel McCluskey, *When Two Become One: Enhancing Sexual Intimacy in Marriage* (Grand Rapids, MI: Revell, 2004), 155.

5. John Eldredge and Stasi Eldredge, *Love and War: Find Your Way to Something Beautiful in Your Marriage* (Colorado Springs, CO: WaterBrook Press, 2011), 178.

6. Gregory Popcak, *Holy Sex! A Catholic Guide to Toe-Curling, Mind-Blowing, Infallible Loving* (New York: Crossroad Publishing Company, 2008), 109.

7. John Paul II, *Man and Woman He Created Them*, 43:2.

8. Gottman, *Seven Principles for Making Marriage Work*, 26. Emphasis added.

9. Kimberly Hahn, *Life-Giving Love: Embracing God's Beautiful Design for Marriage* (Ann Arbor, MI: Charis Books, 2002), 54.

10. Popcak, *Holy Sex!* 24, 145.

8. Understanding the Roots of Conflict

1. Gottman, *Seven Principles of Making Marriage Work*, 28.

2. Gottman, *Seven Principles of Making Marriage Work*, 28.

3. Art Bennett and Laraine Bennett, *The Temperament God Gave You: The Classic Key to Knowing Yourself, Getting Along with Others, and Growing Closer to the Lord* (Manchester, NH: Sophia Institute Press, 2005), 5–6.

4. You can find these resources online at foccusinc.com and prepare-enrich.com.

5. See myersbriggs.org and discprofile.com.

6. John Gray is the author of *Men Are from Mars, Women Are from Venus*. Mary Healy wrote *Men and Women Are from Eden*, based on the Theology of the Body.

7. See Harley, *His Needs, Her Needs* and Gottman, *Seven Principles for Making Marriage Work*.

8. This was in a footnote by the editor Michael Waldstein, in *Male and Female He Created Them: A Theology of the Body*. See also Dr. Larry Crabb's book *Fully Alive*, which describes the meaning and application of these terms.

9. John Paul II, *Letter to Families*.

10. Gottman, *Seven Principles for Making Marriage Work*, 42–45.

11. See Harley, *His Needs, Her Needs*.

12. See Lise Eliot, *Pink Brain, Blue Brain: How Small Differences Grow into Troubling Gaps—and What We Can Do about It* (New York: Mariner Books, 2010).

13. Popcak, *Exceptional Seven Percent*, 117.

14. See Gary Chapman, *The 5 Love Languages: The Secret to Love that Lasts* (Chicago: Northfield Publishing, 2015) for more information on the love languages he identifies.

15. See, for example, Harley, *He Wins, She Wins*.

16. John Paul II, Homily, World Youth Day, July 28, 2002.

9. Healing and Forgiveness

1. Gottman, *Seven Principles of Making Marriage Work*, 32–39.

2. See Richard Rohr, *A Lever and a Place to Stand: The Contemplative Stance, the Active Prayer* (Santa Monica, CA: Hidden Springs Press, 2012).

3. Richard McAlear, *Forgiveness: Experiencing God's Mercy* (Enumclaw, WA: Winepress Publishing, 2006), 11. See also *CCC* 2840.

4. McAlear, *Forgiveness*, 15.

5. If you are interested in learning how to work through these issues, our Healing the Whole Person conferences, workbook, and CDs are available at www.jpiihealingcenter.org.

6. This forgiveness prayer, along with prayers for renouncing judgments, can be found in the Healing the Whole Person training manual at www.jpiihealingcenter.org.

10. Restoring Broken Trust

1. Gary Chapman, *The 4 Seasons of Marriage: Secrets to a Lasting Marriage* (Carol Stream, IL: Tyndale House, 2012), 73.

2. Chapman, *4 Seasons of Marriage*, 78.

3. Chapman, *4 Seasons of Marriage*, 80.

4. The seven A's of a good apology are from Ken Sande, *The Peacemaker: A Biblical Guide to Resolving Personal Conflict* (Grand Rapids, MI: Baker Books, 2004), 126–32.

5. Henry Cloud and John Townsend, *Boundaries in Marriage: Understanding the Choices that Make or Break Loving Relationships* (Grand Rapids, MI: Zondervan, 2002).

Conclusion: A Legacy of Love

1. See *CCC* 1087, 1091, and Bob Schuchts, *Be Transformed: The Healing Power of the Sacraments* (Notre Dame, IN: Ave Maria Press, 2017).

2. Keating, *Spousal Prayer*, 11.

SCRIPTURE   VERSES   9|26|21

ROMANS 12:10 NIV
EPHESIANS 4:29-32

Bob Schuchts is the bestselling author of *Be Healed* and *Be Transformed* and the founder of the John Paul II Healing Center in Tallahassee, Florida.

After receiving his doctorate in family relations from Florida State University in 1981, Schuchts became a teacher and counselor. While in private practice, Schuchts also taught graduate and undergraduate courses at Florida State and Tallahassee Community College. Schuchts later served on faculty at the Theology of the Body Institute and at the Center for Biblical Studies, where he taught courses on healing, sexuality, and marriage. Schuchts also was a guest instructor for the Augustine Institute. He volunteered in parish ministry for more than thirty years.

He retired as a marriage and family therapist in December 2014.

Schuchts has two daughters and eight grandchildren. His wife, Margie, died in 2017.

Christopher West is cofounder, president, and senior lecturer of the Theology of the Body Institute.

Wendy West is cohost of the podcast *Ask Christopher West*.

MORE BOOKS BY
BOB SCHUCHTS

Be Healed
A Guide to Encountering the Powerful Love of Jesus in Your Life

In the tradition of such beloved spiritual teachers as Francis MacNutt and Michael Scanlan, *Be Healed: A Guide to Encountering the Powerful Love of Jesus in Your Life* offers in book form Bob Schuchts's popular program for spiritual, emotional, and physical healing through the power of the Holy Spirit and the sacraments.

Be Transformed
The Healing Power of the Sacraments

Whether it is the wounds of past hurts, the strains in our relationships, or the stresses of daily life, we all need to be comforted and made whole by Christ. Bob Schuchts, whose dynamic healing ministry has brought strength and renewal to thousands, guides you to tap into the power of Christ present in the sacraments and to experience the ongoing effects of their graces in every aspect of your life.